Copycat Recipes

The Complete Step-by-Step Cookbook with Accurate and Tasty Dishes from the Most Famous Restaurants to Make at Home.

Table of Contents

Introduction

The common culinary bond that links cooks throughout Italy is their passion and love for good food, hospitality and tradition. Locally sourced is the name of the game, and it shows in the diversity that you'll find from region to region.

Masterful preparation of sauces that simmer for hours and the patient expertise of kneading dough for homemade bread and pizza are traditional skills that Italian cooks pass down from generation to generation, along with their incredible family recipes.

The tradition of making each meal is a celebration that keeps every Italian cook. When gathering around a table, the family's warmth and vitality is the subtle ingredient that seasons every dish, and love is the spice that's liberally sprinkled to flavor the feast.

Bread

Bread is fundamental and as much a part of the meal as a fork or plate. An Italian table isn't complete until a basket of bread arrives with its earthy, yeasty aroma.

Whether dipped in herb-seasoned olive oil, slathered with butter or used to wipe up every last trace of a fabulous sauce or soup, bread is an integral part of every meal.

The bread recipes of Italy are as varied as the regions from which they come. Chewy, thick-crusted country loaves, herb-infused flat rounds of focaccia and long batons of artisanal breadsticks are some of the traditional bread that is ever-present at the Italian table.

Some regional bread beyond that region's borders and there are even some breeds that baked in a particular town or village.

Antipasto and Appetizers

Translated, Antipasto means "before the meal." The purpose of the Antipasto is to pique the appetite for the meal to follow. It does not mention to fill one up, so plan on allowing one or two of each item per person on your antipasto tray.

Crisp vegetables served with a dip, stuffed vegetables, shrimp or a spicy mixture of vegetables are traditional, although elaborate baked appetizers are also popular.

Other popular ideas are bowls of ripe and green olives, various specialty meats and cheeses or marinated artichoke hearts with roasted red bell peppers. Set out fruits like figs, melons and strawberries to complement the savory foods.

Arrange your Antipasto and appetizers attractively on trays and serve with crusty Italian bread or breadsticks

Gnocchi, Polenta and Rice

In Northern Italy, rice is the starch you'll typically find at your table. It serves as often as pasta is in the southern regions of the country. Just like pasta dishes, risotto is a course in itself. It does not serve as an accompaniment to a meat or fish course.

Gnocchi is another substitute for pasta, and the toothsome little pillows are served with the same type of sauces as you would perform on your favorite pasta. Gnocchi from flour, potato, breadcrumbs or cornmeal, depending upon which region and family tradition you choose.

Polenta is like pasta or rice in that it's a blank canvas for your culinary creations. Whether to create a side dish, serves as a basis for the main course or is studded and garnished with fruits and sweet sauce for dessert, polenta is a humble peasant dish that's perfect for any period of your meal.

Pasta and Sauces

For Italian cooks, pasta is either a meal in itself or a first course. It does not serve as a side dish with meat or vegetables. When saucing pasta, add the drained pasta to the simmering pan of sauce and sauté for a few moments to allow the pasta coated. Never serve pasta swimming in sauce. Use saved pasta cooking water to thin the seasoning if necessary.

As a rule, flat or long noodles are well suited to creamy, smooth sauces. Short, tube-shaped noodles or pasta with ridges and nooks work best with hearty, chunky sauces. The heavy ragu-type sauce is best suited for thick-wall pasta like rigatoni or cavatelli.

Italian sauces run the gamut from a vegetarian seasoning that will delight the most adamant vegan to a meaty concoction to appease the unapologetic carnivore. Don't forget that a pasta sauce doesn't even need to be saucy! It may be a sauté of vegetables in olive oil, a shredding of cheese over steaming hot pasta or even just a drizzle of olive oil with garlic and a grinding of fresh Parmigiano Reggiano.

Pizza

If you start with good dough and the freshest toppings you can find, you're on your way to creating this simple Italian 'fast food.' Just as baking bread takes experience developed over time, you can't rush learning how to make the perfect pizza dough.

Unlike the American penchant for slathering pizza with loads of sauce, the classic Italian pizza with sauce for flavor, so the individual taste of the crust, vegetables, meats and cheeses each shines through.

Pizza crust can range from crisp and thin to thick and chewy, and there are almost limitless topping combinations to please even the pickiest palate.

Egg Dishes

Eggs are quick and easy to prepare, and you'll frequently find them at the luncheon or supper table. However, you're not going to find them on your breakfast plate. Baked eggs and eggs poached in the sauce are simple and tasty ideas for a light lunch. Frittatas are a perfect way to use leftover meats and vegetables and turn simple leftovers into an entirely new and delicious meal.

Soups

The broth is the basis for almost every soup. The broth is easy to make, and it freezes well. If you're serious about making a genuinely marvelous soup, you need to start with flavorful ingredients, and a can of sodium-rich commercial broth just isn't going to do it. Since broth freezes so well, go ahead and make it in large batches so you can freeze individual portions for your future soup adventures.

Italian soups range from delicate creamed or pureed soups, healthy low-calorie vegetable soups, hearty meat soups, elegant seafood soups and stick-to-your-ribs soups enriched with pasta, rice or beans.

Every region has its specialties, and there are innumerable variations on classics like Minestrone and Pasta E Fagioli. Soups with meat or poultry as the main ingredient are rare in Italian cooking. Plan your soups around seasonal fresh local vegetables and use meat as a flavor enhancement rather than the meal's focal point.

Cheese is an essential seasoning for many Italian recipes, so make sure you always have a chunk of Parmigiano Reggiano sitting in the refrigerator, ready to be grated on top of your steaming bowl of soup.

Vegetables

The Italian cook never stocks up on vegetables. For the best dining experience, everything must be fresh from the garden, so shopping for local, seasonal vegetables is an essential part of every cook's daily schedule.

Vegetable dishes are usually simple, and the herbs and spices used in preparing the dish bring out the essence of the freshly picked local ingredients.

Baked vegetables with olive oil and cheese, but many dishes are steamed and garnished with seasonings. Fresh vegetables are usually a part of the Italian dinner table, served with a drizzle of oil and a slice of cheese.

Desserts

Although Gelato and Tiramisu may be the first items that pop into your head when you hear the phrase 'Italian desserts,' there are countless cakes, cookies, puddings and fruit recipes to keep you taste testing for years to come.

Although many specialty dessert recipes are traditional holiday treats, you'll find many simple desserts perfect for any occasion.

Home Cooking Like Restaurant In 6 Steps

Work at home with the efficiency of a chef in a professional kitchen: it is not impossible if you follow a few simple and efficient guidelines. Whether it's preparing daily meals or cooking for a great occasion, organizing kitchen is very important: if everything is clean, neat and organized, work will be easy and fast. This is the approach that restaurants follow (in those that obviously work well) and we want to try copying and exporting to our home.

Of course, some things are impossible: none of us has a team to help them or their professional equipment. However, there are some safety precautions that can be taken just like that to make our movements in the kitchen more efficient. Chef Flavio Forte, a famous and professional chef at Monza Hostaria in Italy, revealed a number of interesting tips. Six secrets that always apply to the concepts of regularity, cleanliness, and attention to quality: many helpful rules, even in a smallest kitchen, that allow you to eat quickly and well.

1) Check your fridge and kitchen before deciding what to cook: knowing what is available can help you work and avoid unpleasant jams.

2) Store food properly so you can always check the product: everything must be stored and tidied up properly. Packed whole, the food is divided by type so you can easily find it; Always separate raw and cooked foods in the refrigerator and freezer. Frozen foods must always be labeled with information and date of preparation.
3) Always work clean: With a clean and tidy working surface and room you can move better, faster and more efficiently. After you are done with the tool, wash and save. Then we know where to find it without wasting time.

4) Arrange the work so that you can do more things together: Prepare the sauce while noodles are being cooked. Season vegetables when meat is browned. Synchronizing at the same time, various actions increases efficiency. Especially if the preliminary work is done beforehand and you have already cleaned and washed vegetables, slices, etc.

5) Use different tools to simplify your work: oven, stove, microwave, blender. Everything you have plays an important role in your kitchen. The preparation time can be shortened by the cooperation of various tools.

6) Choosing quality products makes work easier and improves what you cook. Don't waste time and raw materials with waste, and you are sure you will put something good on your plate.

Tips And Suggestions

Now that you're ready to recreate your favorite restaurant meals at home, you may have wanted to make this a regular part of your culinary adventure. Here are some essential tips and ideas to consider as you progress through this book:

Take your time, and don't rush. Some recipes are quick and can be prepared within minutes, though it's best to slow down and not to hurry at first. You can set aside extra time to create your first meal, to give yourself adequate time. After more than once or two times, you will exactly how much or little time needed to prepare your favorite dishes. Consider the amount of time and effort required to buy groceries, spices, etc. and how you'll want to use these items in your meals. Knowing the importance of using ingredients well and efficiently will encourage you to take your time and avoid wasting them or using too much at once.

Plan your grocery trips to avoid missing ingredients and toppings that you want with your meals. Grocery trips can help you prepare a comprehensive shopping list, with two main categories:

Staple items that only need to be purchased on an "as needed" basis, such as dried goods, pantry items, grains, nuts, seeds, and spices. This may also apply to frozen foods and other items that you may already have many, such as large portions of frozen meat and vegetables.

A second list for seasonal fruits, vegetables, and specialty items that you'll need for the following week, such as perishables (eggs, milk, fruits, and vegetables), and other items that you either need to replenish on a weekly or regular basis.

When you go shopping, bring a list with you and a friend, neighbor, or family member to be both works on selecting ingredients together. Preparing and shopping for food with others is a lovely tradition in some communities, which can be extended to this opportunity.

Invite family and friends to take part in recreating your favorite restaurant meals. They may have some great ideas and suggestions on new meals to prepare and variations to try. It can also be advantageous to include more people in the preparation of recipes. Larger servings and portions make to last longer and feed more people and supplies, and ingredients can be purchased in larger, bulk amounts that are more cost-effective.

When you make your shopping list, include all the basics first, followed by any extras or specialty items for specific recipes or meals. This can be an easy way to stick to your budget and prevent overspending, especially when it is tempting. Many restaurant recipes are made of common ingredients and do not have to be sourced for items not found in most stores or markets. For this reason, shopping for your everyday meals, and these recipes should be simple and easy to manage.

Keep a journal of your experiences in creating your preferred meals and how they turn out. Note any improvements or ideas to change the taste if you have a different preference. For example, some meals are spicy, though some people prefer a savory flavor, and may substitute cayenne or chili powder for paprika or another mild spice. This is also a great way to document your own experience and reflect on which methods you prefer more than others, whether it's switching raw sugar for maple syrup or using almond extract in place of vanilla.

Don't expect each recipe to be perfect the first time! Sometimes the type of oven or a slight change in ingredients can make a significant difference. On other occasions, mistakes can make, or a step is skipped, though it's easy to restart the process and recreate the same dish again, with improvements in place. Never give up, as some recipes can be a bit tricky or challenging at first until you get used to the method.

If you're not sure about a specific recipe, because of it something you've never tried before (either the formula and/ or food), then make a small portion and only buy enough for one batch or meal. This way, you can taste test it for yourself to determine if it's worthwhile to make again. Also, make just enough to sample with friends and family to see how widely it's liked. If you're the only one who likes it, you may only make it once in a while, as a treat, or if your family enjoys it, the recipe may become a more regular meal option.

Prepare your recipe fun and post about it online with friends, family, and co-workers, to share your experience. Communicating and sharing recipes is widely popular. Recreating restaurant meals can be a fun way to connect with people and learn new techniques and options for new and exciting fun adventures. Many people can also learn from their experiences and meals made based on their favorite take-out and dining-in restaurants and fast food outlets.

If you want to make your cooking and baking experience easy and comfortable, make sure you have a good assortment of gravies, sauces, and other go-to mixes in your cupboard. This will ensure that you will have many options to choose from and won't have to worry about making your sauces unless you prefer to make them or the recipe has specific requirements. Hollandaise sauce, gravies, soy sauce, and teriyaki are excellent options to have on hand, just in case you need them in a pinch.

Make a note of any sales or specials in your area at local grocery stores and markets, especially for fresh produce, meat, and dairy. This will give you the best quality at a more affordable price and contribute to your recipes. Making your meals is a satisfying experience, and especially when you can recreate the same meals you enjoy at local restaurants and diners in your neighborhood. This is incredibly fun if you're looking for new items or spices that you may not often purchase as part of your grocery list.

Taking the time to explore new foods and ingredients for your favorite meals is part of the fun in creating these recipes at home. A significant portion of the enjoyment is in anticipation of what's on the menu next, and how much you'll enjoy preparing and savoring the next meal or treat.

Amazing Alfredo

Olive Garden's Fettuccine Alfredo

Olive Garden's classic Fettuccine Alfredo is a simple yet elegant dish. It's easy to make and delicious to eat.

Preparation Time: 5 minutes

Cooking Time: 25 minutes

Servings: 6

Ingredients:

½ cup butter, melted

2 tablespoons cream cheese

1-pint heavy cream

1 teaspoon garlic powder

Some salt

Some black pepper

⅔ Cup parmesan cheese, grated

1-pound fettuccine, cooked

Directions:

Melt the cream cheese in the melted butter over medium heat until soft.

Add the heavy cream and season the mixture with garlic powder, salt, and pepper.

Reduce the heat to low and allow the mixture to simmer for another 15 to 20 minutes.

Remove the mixture from heat and add in the parmesan. Stir everything to melt the cheese.

Pour the sauce over the pasta and serve.

Nutrition:

Calories 679

Total Fat 27.9 g

Carbohydrates 56g

Protein 29.1g

Sodium 233mg

Red Lobster's Shrimp Pasta

Seafood and pasta are always a beautiful combination. Make this at home and enjoy a special meal.

Preparation Time: 5 minutes

Cooking Time: 30 minutes

Servings: 4

Ingredients:

8 ounces linguini or spaghetti pasta

⅓ cup extra virgin olive oil

3 garlic cloves

1-pound shrimp, peeled, deveined

⅔ cup clam juice or chicken broth

⅓ cup white wine

1 cup heavy cream

½ cup parmesan cheese, freshly grated

¼ teaspoon dried basil, crushed

¼ teaspoon dried oregano, crushed

Fresh parsley and parmesan cheese for garnish

Directions:

Cook the pasta according to package directions.

Simmer the garlic in hot oil over low heat, until tender.

Increase the heat to low to medium and add the shrimp. When the shrimp is cooked, transfer it to a separate bowl along with the garlic. Keep the remaining oil in the pan.

Pour the clam or chicken broth into the pan and bring to a boil. Add the wine and adjust the heat to medium. Keep cooking the mixture for another 3 minutes.

While stirring the mixture, reduce the heat to low and add in the cream and cheese. Keep stirring.

When the mixture thickens, return the shrimp to the pan and throw in the remaining ingredients (except the pasta).

Place the pasta in a bowl and pour the sauce over it.

Mix everything together and serve. Garnish with parsley and parmesan cheese, if desired

Nutrition:

Calories 232

Total Fat 14.14g

Carbohydrates 15.5g

Protein 9.2g

Sodium 128mg

Cheesecake Factory's Cajun Jambalaya Pasta

If the last seafood pasta wasn't quite what you were looking for, here is another one that you may like even more.

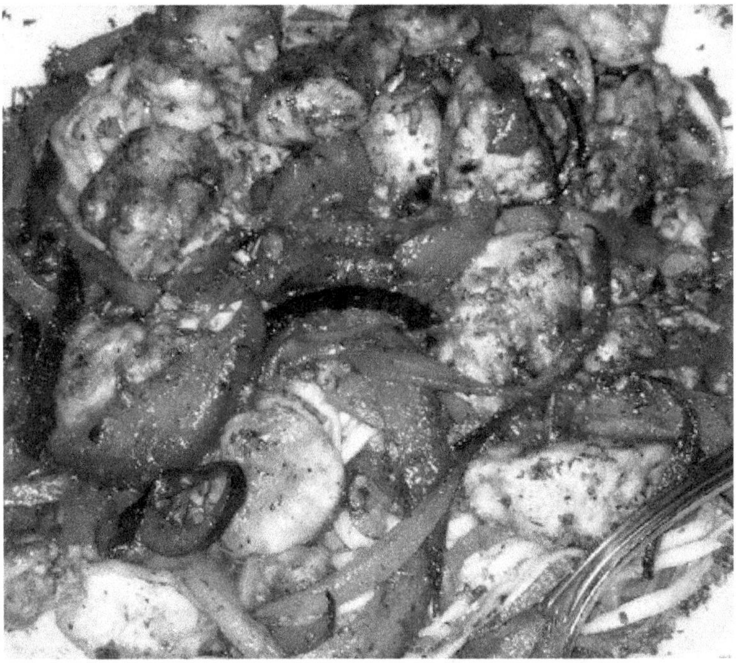

Preparation Time: 10 minutes

Cooking Time: 40 minutes

Servings: 4

Ingredients:

Cajun Seasoning Blend

1 teaspoon white pepper

1 teaspoon cayenne pepper

3 teaspoons salt

1 teaspoon paprika

½ teaspoon garlic powder

½ teaspoon onion powder

Chicken and Shrimp

2 boneless skinless chicken breasts, halved, cut into bite-size pieces

½ pound large shrimp, peeled, deveined

1 tablespoon olive oil

Pasta

5 quarts water

6 ounces fettuccine

6 ounces spinach fettuccine

Jambalaya

1 tablespoon olive oil

2 medium tomatoes, chopped

1 medium onion, sliced

1 green bell pepper, sliced

1 red bell pepper, sliced

1 yellow bell pepper, sliced

1½ cups chicken stock

1 tablespoon cornstarch

2 tablespoons white wine

2 teaspoons arrowroot powder

2 teaspoons fresh parsley, chopped

Directions:

Mix all of the Cajun seasoning blend ingredients in a bowl to make the seasoning. Divide the seasoning into 3 equal parts.

Coat the chicken and shrimp with ⅓ of the seasoning each.

Cook pasta according to package directions.

While waiting for the pasta, sauté the spiced chicken in heated oil in a large skillet.

When the chicken starts turning brown, stir in the shrimp and cook until the chicken is cooked through and shrimp turn pink.

Transfer the chicken and shrimp to a plate and set aside.

Using the same pan, warm the oil for the jambalaya over medium heat. Add the tomatoes, onions, peppers, and remaining 1/3 of the seasoning mix. Sauté for 10 minutes.

When the vegetables turn brownish-black, add the chicken and shrimp back to the mix.

Pour in ¾ cup of the chicken stock to deglaze the pan. Gently scrape the pan to remove the burnt particles. Turn the heat to high and allow the mixture to cook.

When the broth has evaporated completely, add in the remaining stock and cook for another 5 minutes.

Turn the heat down to low and leave the mixture to rest. In a bowl, mix the white wine and arrowroot until it dissolves.

Add the mixture to the jambalaya. Turn the heat to low and leave the mixture to simmer.

When the jambalaya and pasta are done, assemble the dish by putting the pasta as the first layer. Cover the pasta with the jambalaya sauce and garnish with parsley.

Nutrition:

Calories 152

Total Fat 6 g

Carbohydrates 14.56g

Protein 9.45g

Sodium 233 mg

Olive Garden's Steak Gorgonzola

Steak gorgonzola is always delicious. But Olive Garden's pasta brings deliciousness to a whole new level. Make this simple dish at home and enjoy it over a few days.

Preparation Time: 10 minutes

Cooking Time: 1 hour 30 minutes

Servings: 6

Ingredients:

Pasta

2½ pounds boneless beef top sirloin steaks, cut into ½-inch cubes

1-pound fettuccine or linguini, cooked

2 tablespoons sun-dried tomatoes, chopped

2 tablespoons balsamic vinegar glaze

Some fresh parsley leaves, chopped

Marinade

1½ cups Italian dressing

1 tablespoon fresh rosemary, chopped

1 tablespoon fresh lemon juice (optional)

Spinach Gorgonzola Sauce

4 cups baby spinach, trimmed

2 cups Alfredo sauce (recipe follows)

½ cup green onion, chopped

6 tablespoons gorgonzola, crumbled, and divided

Directions:

Cook the pasta and set aside. Mix the marinade ingredients in a sealable container.

Marinate the beef in the container for an hour.

While the beef is marinating, make the Spinach Gorgonzola sauce. Heat the Alfredo sauce in a saucepan over medium heat. Add spinach and green onions. Let simmer until the spinach wilt. Crumble 4 tablespoons of the Gorgonzola cheese on top of the sauce. Let melt and stir. Set aside the remaining 2 tablespoons of the cheese for garnish. Set aside and cover with lid to keep warm.

When the beef is done marinating, grill each piece depending on your preference.

Toss the cooked pasta and the Alfredo sauce in a saucepan, and then transfer to a plate.

Top the pasta with the beef, and garnish with balsamic glaze, sun-dried tomatoes, crumbled gorgonzola cheese, and parsley leaves.

Serve and enjoy.

Nutrition:

Calories 740.5

Total Fat 27.7 g

Carbohydrates 66 g

Protein 54.3 g

Sodium 848.1 mg

Cheesecake Factory's Pasta di Vinci

Nothing is as perfect as pasta with mushrooms. Here's Cheesecake Factory's Pasta Di Vinci—make and eat as much as you like.

Preparation Time: 10 minutes

Cooking Time: 50 minutes

Servings: 4

Ingredients:

½ red onion, chopped

1 cup mushrooms, quartered

2 teaspoons garlic, chopped

1 pound chicken breast, cut into bite-size pieces

3 tablespoons butter, divided

2 tablespoons flour

2 teaspoons salt

¼ cup white wine

1 cup cream of chicken soup mixed with some milk

4 tablespoons heavy cream

Basil leaves for serving, chopped

Parmesan cheese for serving

1-pound penne pasta, cooked, drained

Directions:

Sauté the onion, mushrooms, and garlic in 1 tablespoon of the butter.

When they are tender, remove them from the butter and place in a bowl. Cook the chicken in the same pan.

When the chicken is done, transfer it to the bowl containing the garlic, onions, and mushrooms, and set everything aside.

Using the same pan, make a roux using the flour and remaining butter over low to medium heat. When the roux is ready, mix in the salt, wine, and cream of chicken mixture. Continue stirring the mixture, making sure that it does not burn.

When the mixture thickens, let the mixture simmer for a few more minutes.

Mix in the ingredients that you set aside, and transfer the cooked pasta to a bowl or plate.

Pour the sauce over the pasta, garnish with parmesan cheese and basil, and serve.

Nutrition:

Calories 844.9

Total Fat 35.8 g

Carbohydrates 96.5 g

Protein 33.9 g

Sodium 1400.2 mg

Classic Entrees

Panda Express's Beijing Beef

Beijing beef with crispy marinated beef, bell pepper and sliced onion serves 4 plates and one of the popular Panda express that tons of people craves it.

Preparation time: 20 minutes

Cooking time: 15 minutes

Serving: 4

Ingredients:

1-pound flank steak

1 cup canola oil

4 cloves garlic, minced

1 yellow onion, sliced

1 red bell pepper, cut into 1-inch strips

2 tablespoons + 1 teaspoon cornstarch, divided

¼ teaspoon salt

3 egg whites, beaten

½ cup of water

¼ cup of sugar

3 tablespoons ketchup

6 tablespoons hoisin sauce

1 tablespoon soy sauce

2 teaspoons oyster sauce

4 teaspoons sweet chili sauce

1 teaspoon crushed red peppers

2 tablespoons apple cider vinegar

Directions:

Cut the flank steak against the grain into ¼-inch slices. Place the beef, egg, salt, and 1 teaspoon of cornstarch in a mixing bowl. Cover and refrigerate for at least an hour. In another mixing bowl, whisk together the water, sugar, ketchup, hoisin sauce, soy sauce, oyster sauce, chili sauce, crushed red pepper, and apple cider vinegar. Remove the beef from the refrigerator and place it in a separate dish. Discard the remaining marinade. Sprinkle the beef with 2 tablespoons of cornstarch and stir. Shake off any excess cornstarch. In a medium saucepan, heat the oil over medium-high heat. When hot, fry the beef in batches, about 2–3 minutes. Remove from oil and set on a paper-towel-lined plate to drain. To a large skillet, add 2 tablespoons of the same oil you fried the beef in. Heat over medium-high heat. When hot, add the onion and pepper and cook for about 3 minutes. Add the garlic and cook about 30 seconds more, then remove from the skillet and add to the plate with the beef. Add the sauce you prepared earlier to the skillet and cook over high heat until it thickens. Add the beef and vegetables, stirring to coat.

Nutrition:

Calories 3181 kcal

Protein: 121.62 g

Fat: 253.47 g

Carbohydrates: 104.98 g

Panda Express's Copycat Beef and Broccoli

Brownie stir fried steak beef and broccoli with popular soy sauce gives so much light in this recipe. Such a perfect dinner recipe for you!

Preparation time: 30 minutes

Cooking time: 15 minutes

Serving: 4

Ingredients:

2 tablespoons cornstarch, divided

3 tablespoons Chinese rice wine, divided

1-pound flank steak, cut thinly against the grain

1-pound broccoli florets, chopped into small pieces

2 tablespoons oyster sauce

2 tablespoons water

1 tablespoon brown sugar

1 tablespoon soy sauce

1 tablespoon cornstarch

2 tablespoons canola oil

¼ teaspoon sesame oil

1 teaspoon ginger, finely chopped

2 cloves garlic, finely chopped

2 teaspoons sesame seeds

Directions:

In a large Ziploc bag, add 1 tablespoon cornstarch and 2 tablespoons Chinese rice wine. Place beef inside and seal tightly. Massage bag to fully coat beef. Set aside to marinate for at least 20 minutes.

Rinse broccoli and place in a nonreactive bowl. Place a wet paper towel on top, then microwave for 2 minutes. Set aside.

Stir oyster sauce, water, 1 tablespoon Chinese rice wine, brown sugar, soy sauce, and remaining cornstarch in a bowl until well mixed. Set aside.

Heat wok over high heat. You want the wok to be very hot. Then, heat canola and sesame oil in wok and wait to become hot.

Working in batches, add steak, and cook over high heat for 1 minute. Flip, and cook the other side for another 1 minute. Transfer to a plate.

To the same wok, add garlic and ginger. Sauté for about 10 to 15 seconds then return beef to wok. Toss in cooked broccoli. Slightly stir the prepared sauce to make sure cornstarch is not settled on the bottom, then add to wok. Toss everything in the sauce to combine. Continue cooking until sauce becomes thick. Garnish with sesame seeds. Serve.

Nutrition:

Calories 292 kcal

Protein: 121.19 g

Fat: 66.4 g

Carbohydrates: 53.68

PF Chang's Mongolian Beef

Mongolian Beef is a popular and great home cooked blow-out. Tender beef in pieces covered in a ginger sauce and garlic.

Preparation time: 15 minutes

Cooking time: 10 minutes

Serving: 4-6

Ingredients:

1 cup of vegetable oil

1½ pounds flank steak

½ cup cornstarch

¼ teaspoon red pepper flakes (optional)

One bunch green onion, diagonal cut into 2-inch pieces

Rice for serving

Sauce

1 tablespoon vegetable oil

1–2 teaspoons ginger, minced

1 tablespoon garlic, minced

½ cup of soy sauce

½ cup of water

¾ cup dark brown sugar

Directions:

Prepare the sauce by heating the oil in a medium saucepan over medium-high heat. Add the ginger and garlic. Stir and cook for about 30 seconds.

Add the soy sauce, water, and brown sugar. Bring mixture to a boil, then reduce heat slightly and allow to simmer until the sauce begins to thicken.

Prepare steak by slicing it into ¼-inch slices, working against the grain to keep it tender. Place the cornstarch in a shallow dish, then dredge the sliced beef in the cornstarch to coat, shaking off any excess.

While the beef sits, heat the oil in a skillet over medium-high heat. When hot, add the beef and cook for about 3 minutes or until brown and crisp. Make sure to cook on both sides.

Remove the beef from the skillet and place on a plate. Drain the oil from the skillet and put the beef back in. Add the sauce and cook, stirring to make sure the beef is covered with sauce.

Sprinkle in the red pepper flakes and green onions.

Remove from heat and serve with rice.

Nutrition:

Calories 212 kcal

Protein: 167.65 g

Fat: 295.68 g

Carbohydrates: 221.92 g

PF Chang's Beef A La Sichuan

Tossed with a spicy sauce and veggies for those who are not familiar with this special dish – fried strips of beef. Easy to make at home.

Preparation time: 20 minutes

Cooking time: 10 minutes

Serving: 4-6

Ingredients:

Stir-fry

1-pound flank steak or sirloin, sliced thin

4 medium celery ribs

2 medium carrots

1 green onion

¼ cup peanut oil or canola oil

¼ cup cornstarch

½ teaspoon red pepper flakes

1½ teaspoons sesame oil

Sauce

3 tablespoons soy sauce

2 tablespoons hoisin sauce

1 tablespoon garlic and red chili paste

½ teaspoon Chinese hot mustard

One teaspoon rice wine vinegar

½ teaspoon chili oil

2 teaspoons brown sugar

1 teaspoon garlic, minced

½ teaspoon fresh ginger, minced

½ teaspoon red pepper flakes

Directions:

Whisk together all of the sauce ingredients in a mixing bowl. Set aside. Slice the carrots and celery as thinly as possible and set aside. Place the sliced beef in a medium bowl and sprinkle it with the cornstarch. Make sure every piece is coated. Allow sitting for 10 minutes. Heat the oil in a large skillet or wok over medium-high heat and cook the beef until crispy, about 4–5 minutes. When done, remove beef from the oil to a paper-towel-lined plate to drain. Discard any oil remaining in the skillet. Add the sesame oil to the same skillet and heat over high heat. Add the celery, stir, and cook for about 1 minute. Add the crushed red pepper and stir. Add the carrots, cooking and stirring for another 30 seconds. Add the beef and green onions and stir, then pour the sauce into the skillet and bring to a boil. Allow to cook for one more minute, then serve over rice.

Nutrition:

Calories 1730 kcal

Protein: 112.13 g

Fat: 102.9 g

Carbohydrates: 84.99 g

Southwest Steak

Grilled southwest steak with vegetables is your next memorable family dinner with this recipe.

Preparation time: 20 minutes

Cooking time: 10 minutes

Serving: 2

Ingredients:

2 (6-ounce) sirloin steaks, or your favorite cut

2 teaspoons blackened steak seasoning

½ cup red peppers, sliced

½ cup green peppers, sliced

2 tablespoons unsalted butter

1 cup yellow onion, sliced

2 cloves garlic, minced

Salt, to taste

Pepper, to taste

2 slices cheddar cheese

2 slices Monterey jack cheese

Vegetable medley or/and garlic mashed potatoes, for serving.

Directions:

Preheat a cast-iron (or other heavy skillets) or a grill.

Season the meat with steak seasoning and cook to your desired doneness (about 3–4 minutes on each side for medium-rare).

In another skillet, melt the butter and cook the peppers, onion, and garlic. Season with salt and pepper.

Before the steak has reached your desired doneness, top with a slice of each cheese and cook a bit longer until it melts.

Serve the steaks with pepper and onion mix and garlic mashed potatoes.

Nutrition:

Calories 627 kcal

Protein: 24.31 g

Fat: 49.52 g

Carbohydrates: 21.71 g

Chicken Fingers

Craving some bite of chicken fingers? Here's a perfect choice of recipe to make at your home.

Preparation time: 20 minutes

Cooking time: 10minutes

Serving: 6

Ingredients:

6 boneless skinless chicken breasts, cut into strips

1 egg, beaten

1 cup buttermilk

1 ½ teaspoon garlic powder

1 cup all-purpose flour

1 cup seasoned bread crumbs

1 teaspoon salt

1 teaspoon baking powder

1-quart oil, for frying

Honey Mustard Sauce

¼ cup mayonnaise

¼ cup Dijon mustard

¼ cup honey

1 tablespoon yellow mustard

1 tablespoon vinegar

⅛ teaspoon paprika

French fries, for serving.

Directions:

Start by making the honey mustard sauce. Combine all the ingredients in a bowl, whisk, and set it in the refrigerator until you are ready.

Place the chicken breast strips in a resealable bag.

In a mixing bowl, combine the egg, buttermilk, and garlic powder and stir to combine. Pour this mixture over the chicken in the bag, and refrigerate for at least 2 hours.

In another large bag or shallow dish, combine the flour, bread crumbs, salt, and baking powder.

After the chicken has marinated, remove it from the refrigerator. Discard the extra buttermilk mixture.

Place the chicken pieces one or two at a time into the flour and bread crumb bag. Shake the bag to coat the chicken thoroughly.

Heat the oil in a large skillet to 375°F and carefully place the chicken in the hot oil. Cook until the outside is golden-brown, and the chicken is cooked through.

Place the pieces on a paper towel-lined plate to drain.

Serve with honey mustard sauce and French fries.

Nutrition:

Calories 1375 kcal

Protein: 47.05 g

Fat: 42 g

Carbohydrates: 205.41 g

Fiesta Lime Chicken

A 20 minutes recipe is not bad for your dinner. Fiesta lime chicken topped with Mexican rice and melted cheese!

Preparation time: 10 minutes

Cooking time: 20 minutes

Serving: 4

Ingredients:

4 boneless skinless chicken breasts

2 tablespoons olive oil

Salt and pepper to taste

¼ cup ranch dressing

¼ cup Greek yogurt

1 tablespoon lime juice

¼ cup fresh cilantro chopped

1 clove garlic, minced

½ cup Colby cheese, shredded

½ cup Monterey jack cheese, shredded

For serving

Mexican Rice

Pico de Gallo

Tortilla strips

Directions:

Preheat the grill or the oven to 400°F.

Brush the chicken breasts with olive oil, then season with salt and pepper as desired.

Grill the chicken for about 10 minutes on each side, or bake for 20 minutes in the oven, until it is cooked through and the juices run clear.

In a mixing bowl, combine the ranch dressing, yogurt, lime juice, cilantro, and garlic. Stir well.

Just before the chicken is done, spread a bit of the dressing mixture over each breast and top with a portion of the cheeses. Continue to cook until the cheese is melted.

To serve, plate a scoop of Mexican rice and place a chicken breast on top. Add Pico de Gallo and tortilla strips.

Nutrition:

Calories 1244 kcal

Protein: 44 g

Fat: 103.86 g

Carbohydrates: 36.31 g

Margherita Chicken

This easy skinless chicken breast with melted cheese is a great meal for you. Delicious meal recipe that can be easily cook within 25 minutes at your home.

Preparation time: 20 minutes

Cooking time: 25 minutes

Serving: 4

Ingredients:

4 boneless skinless chicken breasts

Spice rub

2 tablespoons packed brown sugar

Juice of 1 lime

1 tablespoon oil

2 tablespoons paprika

1 tablespoon chili powder

1 tablespoon ground cumin

1 ½ teaspoons salt

1 teaspoon pepper

Glaze

½ cup ketchup

¼ cup balsamic vinegar

1 teaspoon oregano

¼ cup packed brown sugar

Cheese topping

1 cup mozzarella cheese, shredded

½ cup Parmesan cheese, grated

Bruschetta

2 cloves garlic, chopped

2 teaspoons balsamic vinegar

½ teaspoon kosher salt

¼ teaspoon fresh cracked pepper

2 tablespoons chopped fresh basil

3 tablespoons olive oil

6 Roma tomatoes, diced

Directions:

Combine all the rub ingredients and spread the mixture over the chicken, using your fingers to massage it into the meat. Cover the chicken with wrap and refrigerate for at least an hour.

When the chicken is almost done marinating, make the bruschetta. Combine the garlic, vinegar, salt, pepper, and basil in a small bowl. Stir to combine. Slowly whisk in the olive oil, then add the tomatoes. Cover with plastic wrap and set aside until you are ready to assemble.

In a small bowl, mix all together with the glaze ingredients.

After your chicken has marinated, preheat the grill and set the oven to broil. Cook the chicken over medium-high heat until the juices run clear, and the meat has an internal temperature of 165°F. While the chicken is cooking, occasionally brush glaze over the breasts but watch them carefully so they don't burn.

When chicken is done on the grill, place it on a baking tray and top it with both the mozzarella and Parmesan cheeses. Set them below the broiler and cook until the cheese is melty and a bit bubbly.

Serve the chicken topped with the bruschetta topping.

Nutrition:

Calories 1650 kcal

Protein: 70.62 g

Fat: 80.16 g

Carbohydrates: 180.9 g

Shrimp and Parmesan Steak

Want to try this delicious shrimp and parmesan steak with fresh veggies in your house? Go to your kitchen and try this cheesy steak now!

Preparation time: 5 minutes

Cooking time: 20 minutes

Serving: 2

Ingredients:

1 cup heavy cream

½ cup Parmesan cheese, grated

2 teaspoons dried basil

Salt and pepper to taste

2 (8 ounces) ribeye steaks

8 ounces shrimp (or prawns), peeled, deveined, and tails removed

1 tablespoon butter, melted

Directions:

Preheat your grill. You can cook these on the stovetop, but the smoky flavor added to the dish by grilling brings the best flavor.

Over medium-low heat, put the heavy cream to a simmer in a saucepan

After you have reached a simmer, stir in the cheese and basil and season with salt and pepper. Lower the heat to remain the sauce warm while you cook the shrimp and the steak.

Spice the steaks with salt and pepper (or whatever spices you like on your meat). Grill for about 4 minutes on each side or to your desired doneness.

Cook the shrimp on the grill for about 40 seconds to a minute on each side, basting with melted butter.

To serve, put a steak on each serving plate. Top with grilled shrimp and a scoop of the Parmesan sauce.

Nutrition:

Calories 1987 kcal

Protein: 167.64 g

Fat: 135.9 g

Carbohydrates: 23.95 g

Mesa Grill's Crusted Filet Mignon

Make your weekend day with this hot smoked crusted filet mignon – a simple recipe. A perfect way for your lunch to fill your steak cravings.

Preparation time: 20 minutes

Cooking time: 8 minutes

Serving: 4

Ingredients:

Roasted Red Pepper and Ancho Salsa

2 ancho chiles

½ cup boiling water

4 cloves garlic, chopped

2 tablespoons pine nuts

1 tablespoon honey

2 roasted red bell peppers, stripped

2 tablespoons red wine vinegar

3 tablespoons cut fresh cilantro leaves

½ teaspoon salt

¼ teaspoon ground black pepper

For the Steak

4 (8-ounce) filet mignon steaks

1 tablespoon vegetable oil

½ teaspoon salt

4 teaspoons black pepper, coarsely

8 ounces fresh goat cheese, cut into 4 slices

Cilantro leaves, for garnish

Directions:

Prepare the salsa. Pour the boiling water over the ancho chilies and let it sit for 1 hour. Remove the chilies from the water (keep the water) and chop the chilies, discarding the stems and seeds. Place them in a blender with ¼ cup of the soaking liquid, the garlic, pine nuts, and honey. Process until smooth. In a medium bowl, combine the purée with the bell peppers, red wine vinegar, cilantro, salt, and pepper. Cover the bowl and keep it at room temperature for 1 hour, or up to 4 hours. Heat the grill to medium-high. Clean and oil the grates. Brush the steaks with oil. Sprinkle both sides with salt and press the peppercorns into one side of each steak. When the grill is hot, cook the steaks pepper side down for about 3 minutes, until the pepper is nicely charred. Turn over the steaks and cook them another 4 minutes or so on the other side (for medium-rare, internal temperature measures 135°F). In the final minute of cooking, place a slice of cheese on top of each steak, and allow it to melt a bit. Rest the steak for 5–10 minutes before serving. Plate each steak and top with the Red Pepper Ancho salsa.

Nutrition:

Calories 3465 kcal

Protein: 244.75 g

Fat: 246.71 g

Carbohydrates: 58.81 g

Texas Roadhouse's Red Chili

Texas roadhouse's red chili is a meat and flavorful topped with favorite cheese for your dinner.

Preparation time: 20 minutes

Cooking time: 1 hour

Serving: 6

Ingredients:

2 tablespoons vegetable oil

2 pounds beef chuck, cut into bite-sized cubes

1 yellow onion, diced

2 cloves garlic, chopped

1 ½ teaspoon chili powder

1 teaspoon ground cumin

1 teaspoon paprika

1 teaspoon salt

½ teaspoon black pepper

¼ teaspoon red pepper flakes

1 tablespoon brown sugar

1 ½ cups crushed tomatoes

2 teaspoons white vinegar

1 (15-ounce) can red kidney beans

2 jalapeños, seeded and sliced

Optional for topping

Shredded cheddar

Green onions, chopped

Directions:

Heat the oil and cook the meat well in a saucepan.

Add the onion and cook to soften, and then stir in the garlic and cook until fragrant.

Add the chili powder, cumin, paprika, salt, pepper, red pepper flakes, and brown sugar. Mix to combine.

Stir in the crushed tomatoes and vinegar. Set the pot to a simmer, cover, and cook for 30 minutes.

Add the kidney beans and jalapeños and cook 10 more minutes.

Serve hot with a sprinkle of shredded cheese and green onion.

Nutrition:

Calories 2335 kcal

Protein: 232.49 g

Fat: 139.91 g

Carbohydrates: 43.17 g

Texas Roadhouse's Rattlesnake Bites

Texas roadhouse's Rattlesnake Bites are so good!

Preparation time: 15 minutes

Cooking time: 30 minutes

Serving: 6

Ingredients:

1 c. shredded mozzarella

1 c. Shredded Monterey Jack

2 jalapeños, minced

1 clove garlic, minced

1 c. all-purpose flour

kosher salt

Freshly ground black pepper

3 large eggs, beaten

1 c. plain bread crumbs

1 tsp. paprika

1/2 tsp. garlic powder

1/2 tsp. cayenne pepper

Canola or vegetable oil, for frying

Ranch dressing, for serving

Directions:

Line a large, rimmed baking sheet with parchment. In a large bowl, mix together cheeses, jalapeños, and garlic.

Using a tablespoon, scoop into balls and squeeze tight. Place on baking sheet and freeze until solid, at least 30 minutes.

Set up dredging station: In a shallow bowl, add flour and season with salt and pepper. In another shallow bowl, add eggs. In a third shallow bowl, add bread crumbs, paprika, garlic powder, and cayenne. Mix to combine.

Roll frozen cheese balls into flour, then eggs, and then bread crumbs, repeating until all are well coated.

In a large, deep skillet, heat 1/4" oil over medium heat until shimmering. In batches, fry bites until golden on all sides, about 3 minutes. Drain on paper towels.

Serve bites with ranch.

Nutrition:

Calories 1375 kcal

Protein: 47.05 g

Fat: 42 g

Carbohydrates: 205.41 g

Chili's Baby Back Ribs

Tender Chili's baby back ribs covered with a specialty recipe then grilled for 3 hours and 30 minutes. A perfect meal to share with your friends and family.

Preparation time: 15 minutes

Cooking time: 3 hours and 30 minutes

Serving: 4

Ingredients:

Pork

4 racks baby-back pork ribs

Sauce

1½ cups water

1 cup white vinegar

½ cup tomato paste

1 tablespoon yellow mustard

⅔ cup dark brown sugar packed

1 teaspoon hickory flavored liquid smoke

1½ teaspoons salt

½ teaspoon onion powder

¼ teaspoon garlic powder

¼ teaspoon paprika

Directions:

Mix all of the sauce ingredients and then bring to a boil.

When the sauce starts to boil, reduce it to a simmer. Continue simmering the mixture for 45 to 60 minutes, mixing occasionally. When the sauce is almost done, preheat the oven to 300°F.

Choose a flat surface and lay some aluminum foil over it to cover 1 rack of ribs. Place the ribs on top.

Remove the sauce from heat and start brushing it all over the ribs.

When the rack is completely covered, wrap it with the aluminum foil and place it on the baking pan with the foil's opening facing upwards.

Repeat steps 3 to 5 for the remaining racks.

Bake the ribs for 2½ hours.

When they are almost done baking, preheat your grill to medium heat.

Grill both sides of each rack for 4 to 8 minutes. When you are almost done grilling, brush some more sauce over each side and grill for a few more minutes. Make sure that the sauce doesn't burn.

Transfer the racks to a large plate and serve with extra sauce.

Nutrition:

Calories 1635 kcal

Protein: 176.65 g

Fat: 52.42 g

Carbohydrates: 98.55 g

Taco Bell's Crunchwrap Supreme

Treat yourself to Taco Bell in the comfort of your own home!

Preparation time: 20 minutes

Cooking time: 40 minutes

Serving: 4

Ingredients:

FOR THE CRUNCHWRAP

4 frozen hash brown patties

5 large eggs

1 tbsp. whole milk

1 tbsp. butter

kosher salt

Freshly ground black pepper

2 tbsp. finely chopped chives

4 large flour tortillas

6 slices cooked bacon, chopped

1 c. shredded Cheddar

1 c. Shredded Monterey Jack

Vegetable oil, for pan

FOR THE CREAMY JALAPEÑO SAUCE

1/3 c. sour cream

Juice of 1/2 lime

1 jalapeño, minced

1/4 tsp. paprika

kosher salt

Freshly ground black pepper

Directions:

Bake frozen hash brown patties according to package instructions.

Make creamy jalapeño sauce: In a small bowl, whisk together sour cream, lime juice, jalapeño and paprika, then season with salt and pepper. Set aside.

Meanwhile, make scrambled eggs: In a large bowl, combine eggs and milk and whisk until frothy. In a medium nonstick pan, melt butter over medium heat. Pour egg mixture into the pan. Let set slightly then reduce heat to medium-low. Drag the eggs with a spatula or wooden spoon to create curds. When the eggs are almost cooked to your liking, season with salt and pepper. Fold in chives and remove from heat.

Assemble crunchwrap: Spread the jalapeño sauce onto the center of each flour tortilla, then top each with a hash brown patty, scrambled eggs, bacon, cheddar and Monterey Jack. Fold tortillas around the center, creating pleats. After wrapping, quickly invert crunchwraps so the pleats are on the bottom and they stay together.

Cook crunchwraps: In a medium nonstick pan over medium heat, heat a very thin layer of vegetable oil. Working one at a time, add crunchwrap seam-side down and cook until tortilla is golden on the bottom, 3 to 5 minutes. Flip crunchwrap and cook until the other side is golden, 3 to 5 minutes more.

Repeat with remaining crunchwraps. Cut each in half and serve warm.

Nutrition:

Calories 1635 kcal

Protein: 176.65 g

Fat: 52.42 g

Carbohydrates: 98.55 g

Soups And Salads

Copycat Olive Garden's Creamy Zuppa Toscana

A super easy Olive Garden's Creamy Zuppa Toscana is a hot Italian sausage with sliced bacon and fresh spinach. Try this creamy and flavorful soup!

Preparation Time: 25 minutes

Cooking Time: 1 hour

Servings: 6

Ingredients:

1-pound Italian sausage, ground

1¼ teaspoon red pepper flakes, ground

4 bacon slices, cut into ½-inch pieces

1 large onion, diced

1 tablespoon minced garlic

5 13¾-ounce cans chicken broth

6 potatoes, finely chopped

1 cup heavy cream

2 cups fresh spinach leaves

Directions:

In a large pot, cook sausage and red pepper flakes on medium-high heat for at least 10 minutes or until brown. Drain. Transfer to a bowl and set aside.

In the same pot, cook bacon on medium heat for 10 minutes or until crunchy. Drain drippings until only a few tablespoons are left at the bottom of the pot. Mix in onions and garlic with the bacon. Cook for 5 minutes or until onions are tender.

Add chicken broth into the pot and adjust heat to high. Bring to a boil. Add potatoes and boil for 20 minutes. Adjust heat to medium and mix in cream and cooked sausage to reheat.

Stir in spinach and serve.

Nutrition:

Calories 554

Total Fat 33 g

Carbohydrates 46 g

Protein 20 g

Sodium 2386 mg

Panera's Broccoli Cheddar Soup

Panera's Broccoli cheddar soup is a creamy and simple yet good enough to serve for late-night weekend.

Preparation Time: 15 minutes

Cooking Time: 50 minutes

Servings: 8

Ingredients:

1 tablespoon butter

½ onion, diced

¼ cup melted butter

¼ cup flour

2 cups milk

2 cups chicken stock

1½ cup broccoli florets, diced

1 cup carrots, cut into thin strips

1 stalk celery, sliced

2½ cups Cheddar cheese, grated

Salt and pepper, to taste

Directions:

Melt 1 tablespoon of butter in a skillet and cook onion over medium heat for 5 minutes or until caramelized. Set aside.

In a saucepan, mix melted butter and flour, then cook on medium-low heat. Add 1 or 2 tablespoons milk to the flour to prevent from burning. Cook for at least 3 minutes or until smooth.

While stirring, gently pour the rest of the milk in with the flour. Mix in chicken stock. Simmer for 20 minutes or until thick and well blended. Toss in broccoli, carrots, cooked onion, and celery. Cook for an additional 20 minutes or until vegetables turn soft.

Mix in cheese and stir until the cheese is completely melted. Season with salt and pepper, to taste.

Transfer into individual bowls. Serve.

Nutrition:

Calories 304

Total Fat 23 g

Carbohydrates11 g

Protein 14 g

Sodium 624 mg

Panera's Autumn Squash Soup

Panera has a cult following around their soups and especially their autumn squash soup.

Preparation Time: 20 minutes

Cooking Time: 40 minutes

Servings: 6

Ingredients:

2 tbsp. extra-virgin olive oil

1 (2-lb.) butternut squash, peeled, and seeded, and cut into 1" cubes

2 medium carrots, peeled and chopped

2 large shallots, chopped

Kosher salt

Freshly ground black pepper

2 cloves garlic, minced

1 tbsp. packed brown sugar

2 tsp. ground ginger

1 tsp. curry powder

4 c. low-sodium vegetable broth

1 c. apple juice

1 c. water

1/2 c. pumpkin puree

2 tbsp. cream cheese, softened

Heavy cream (optional)

FOR THE TOPPING

1 tbsp. extra-virgin olive oil

1/2 c. pepitas

1/2 tsp. chili powder

Kosher salt

Directions:

In a large pot over medium heat, heat oil. Add squash, carrots, and shallots and season with salt and pepper. Cook, stirring occasionally, until beginning to soften, about 5 minutes. Stir in garlic, sugar, ginger, and curry powder, and cook until vegetables are beginning to caramelize, about 2 minutes more.

Pour over broth, apple juice, and water. Bring to a boil, then reduce to a simmer and cook until vegetables are soft, about 10 minutes.

Meanwhile, in a small bowl, whisk together pumpkin puree and cream cheese until incorporated.

Pour pumpkin mixture into pot and stir to combine.

Using an immersion blender, puree soup until smooth. Season with salt and pepper and stir in desired amount of heavy cream, if using. Serve soup topped with pepitas.

FOR THE TOPPING

Preheat oven to 350°. On a medium baking sheet, toss pepitas with oil and chili powder and season with salt.

Bake, shaking the pan halfway through, until pepitas are crunchy and golden, about 10 minutes.

Let cool completely.

Nutrition:

Calories 304

Total Fat 23 g

Carbohydrates11 g

Protein 14 g

Sodium 624 mg

Outback's Baked Potato Soup

A cheesy baked potato soup that is easy to make and taste like heaven. The flavors are so smooth and creamy that you can't resist to eat every meal. Now you can serve the outback's baked potato soup at home.

Preparation Time: 5 minutes

Cooking Time: 40 minutes

Servings: 8

Ingredients:

2 quarts water

8 medium-sized potatoes, cut into chunks

4 cans chicken broth

1 small onion, minced

1 teaspoon salt

1 teaspoon ground pepper

2 cups cold water

1 cup butter

¾ cup flour

1½ cup heavy cream

1½ cups jack cheese

2-3 thick-cut bacon slices, cooked and diced

¼ cup green onion, minced

Directions:

In a pot, add water and potatoes. Bring to a boil, reduce heat to medium and cook potatoes for 10-15 minutes or until for tender. Drain and set aside.

In a separate pot, pour in broth and mix in onions, salt, pepper, and water. Simmer for 20 minutes.

Meanwhile, in another pot, whisk together butter and flour. Slowly add this to the pot of broth. Stir in heavy cream to the mixture and simmer for 20 minutes. Mix in potatoes to reheat. Sprinkle jack cheese, bacon bits, and green onions on top. Serve.

Nutrition:

Calories 845

Total Fat 49 g

Carbs 81 g

Protein 23 g

Sodium 1652 mg

Copycat Pasta e Fagioli from Olive Garden

A super simple and convenient recipe that taste better than fast food place – pasta e fagioli from olive garden.

Preparation Time: 10 minutes

Cooking Time: 20 minutes

Servings: 8

Ingredients:

1 cup ditalini pasta

2 tablespoons olive oil, divided

1-pound Italian sausage

3 garlic cloves, finely chopped

1 onion, chopped

3 carrots, peeled and chopped

2 stalks celery, chopped

3 cups chicken broth

1 16-ounce can tomato sauce

1 15-ounce can dice tomatoes

1 teaspoon dried basil

1 teaspoon dried oregano

¾ teaspoon dried thyme

1 cup water

Salt and pepper, to taste

1 15-ounce can red kidney beans, drained and rinsed

Directions:

Cook pasta following the instructions on the package. Drain and set aside.

Add 1 tablespoon oil to a pot and heat. Sauté sausage in pot for at least 3 minutes or until brown over medium heat. Drain and set aside.

Heat the rest of the oil in the same pot over medium-low heat. Add garlic, onion, carrots, and celery. Mix from time to time while cooking for at least 3 minutes or until vegetables soften.

Pour in broth, tomato sauce, tomatoes, basil, oregano, thyme, cooked sausage, and water. Add salt and pepper, to taste. Once boiling, adjust heat to low and let simmer for another 10 minutes or until all vegetables are soft.

Mix in cooked pasta and beans to reheat.

Top with shaved parmesan cheese if desired and serve.

Nutrition:

Calories 340

Total Fat 10 g

Carbs 44 g

Protein 22 g

Sodium 889 mg

Panera's Lemon Chicken Orzo Soup

A delicious and soothing mix of tender chicken, ginger, spices and pasta orzo.

Preparation Time: 20 minutes

Cooking Time: 1 hour

Servings: 12

Ingredients:

Water, for boiling

Salt, to taste

8 ounces orzo pasta

1 teaspoon olive oil

3 carrots, diced

3 ribs celery, diced

1 onion, diced

2 cloves garlic, finely chopped

½ teaspoon dried thyme

½ teaspoon dried oregano

Salt, to taste

Pepper, to taste

1 bay leaf

3 32-ounce cartons chicken broth

½ cup fresh lemon juice

1 lemon, zested

8 ounces cooked chicken breast, diced

1 8-ounce package baby spinach leaves

1 lemon, sliced

¼ cup Parmesan cheese, shredded

Directions:

Add water and a bit of salt to a pot and bring to a boil. Add orzo and cook for about 5 minutes, or until pasta is al dente. Remove from heat. Drain, then run under cold water until cool.

In a large pot, heat olive oil over medium heat. Add carrots, celery, and onion. Sauté for about 5 to 7 minutes until vegetables become tender and onion is translucent. Stir in garlic. Cook for another minute or until aromatic. Toss in thyme, oregano, salt, black pepper, and bay leaf. Cook for an additional 30 seconds, then add chicken broth. Bring to a boil. Bring heat to medium-low. Simmer for about 10 minutes or until all vegetables are soft.

Add orzo and lemon zest. Pour in lemon juice and the chicken. Cook everything for about 3 minutes until both the chicken and orzo are heated thoroughly. Toss in spinach and cook for about 2 to 3 minutes. The soup is ready once the spinach wilts into the broth and the orzo is soft.

Transfer into bowls and serve with lemon slices and Parmesan cheese.

Nutrition:

Calories 167

Total fat 4 g

Saturated fat 2 g

Carbs 22 g

Sugar 4 g

Fibers 3 g

Protein 12 g

Sodium 187 mg

DIY California Quinoa Salad from Whole Foods

A quick and colorful recipe that taste better than restaurant is a refreshing and perfect meal.

Preparation Time: 10 minutes

Cooking Time: 10 minutes

Servings: 4

Ingredients:

2 cups water

1 cup quinoa

¼ cup balsamic vinegar

2 tablespoons lime zest

1 mango, peeled and finely chopped

1 red bell pepper, finely chopped

½ cup pre-cooked edamame, peeled

⅓ cup red onion, diced

¼ cup unsweetened coconut flakes

¼ cup almonds, chopped

¼ cup raisins

2 tablespoons cilantro leaves, diced

Directions:

In a skillet, cook quinoa with water according to package instructions.

Meanwhile, combine balsamic vinegar and lime zest in a bowl.

In a separate bowl, mix together cooked quinoa, mango, bell pepper, edamame, red onion, coconut flakes, almonds, raisins, and cilantro.

Add vinegar and lime zest sauce onto quinoa salad. Toss to coat salad.

Serve.

Nutrition:

Calories 351

Total Fat 10 g

Carbs 57 g

Protein 11 g

Sodium 17 mg

Olive Garden's Salad and Creamy Dressing

Try our olive garden's salad and creamy dressing yourself. Making your own salad is better than ordering in a restaurant.

Preparation Time: 15 minutes

Cooking Time: 0 minutes

Servings: 4

Ingredients:

Dressing:

1 cup mayonnaise

⅔ cup white vinegar

5 teaspoons granulated sugar

2 tablespoons lemon juice

1 tablespoon water

⅔ cup Parmesan-Romano cheese blend

2 teaspoons olive oil

1 teaspoon Italian seasoning

1 teaspoon parsley flakes

½ teaspoon garlic salt

Salad

1 bag salad blend of choice

Red onion, sliced

16-20 pitted black olives, sliced

Pepperoncini

Roma tomato, sliced

Croutons

Parmesan cheese, shredded

Directions:

To make the dressing, add mayonnaise, white vinegar, sugar, lemon juice, water, cheese blend, olive oil, Italian seasoning, parsley, and garlic salt to a blender. Pulse until well combined. Store in refrigerator. Ready to serve after at least 2 hours.

Assemble salad by layering salad blend, red onion, black olives, pepperoncini, tomato, croutons, and Parmesan cheese in a bowl.

Serve.

Nutrition:

Calories 649

Total fat 57 g

Saturated fat 15 g

Carbs 16 g

Sugar 6 g

Fibers 1 g

Protein 18 g

Sodium 1309 mg

KFC Coleslaw

You can make homemade coleslaw that tastes even better than KFC.

Preparation Time: 5 minutes

Cooking Time: 0 minutes

Servings: 4

Ingredients:

13 cups chopped cabbage This is about 1 large head of cabbage or 2 medium heads of cabbage

1 green bell pepper (optional, there is no bell pepper in the KFC recipe)

1/2 cup choped onion

1/2 cup chopped carrot 1 medium size carrot

2 cups Miracle Whip Light

1/2 cup sugar

1/4 cup vinegar

1/4 cup vegetable oil

Directions:

If you are lucky enough to have a food processor, get it out of your cupboard. Start to cut up the cabbage and place it in the processor. While cutting up the cabbage, also cut up small slices of green pepper, onion, and carrot and add to the processor.

Mixing up the ingredients this way will help distribute the flavors throughout the slaw. You may want to use a little less of the onion, or green bell pepper, but do use all of the carrot. If you do not have a food processor, no problem, simply chop the cabbage, onions, and carrots into small pieces. Add chopped green bell pepper if desired.

Now mix Miracle Whip, vinegar, oil, and sugar until you have a smooth mixture. The taste should be sweet with just a hint of vinegar.

Amount of dressing may be increased or decreased according to the amount of slaw you are making. Add to cut up veggies and mix well. Let stand at least one hour to let flavors mix.

Nutrition:

Calories 177

Total fat 10 g

Saturated fat 1 g

Carbs 21 g

Sugar 15 g

Fiber 2 g

Protein 1 g

Sodium 355 mg

Panera Bread Black Bean Soup

You can make homemade Panera Bread Black Bean Soup

Preparation Time: 20 minutes

Cooking Time: 60 minutes

Servings: 8

Ingredients:

1 cup white onion chopped

1/2 cup celery chopped

1/2 cup carrot chopped

2 tablespoons vegetable oil

1/2 cup chopped red bell pepper

2 teaspoons minced garlic

32 ounces vegetable stock

30 ounces black beans or 3 to 4 cups of cooked black beans

1 to 2 teaspoons salt

1 to 2 teaspoons cumin

1 1/2 teaspoon lemon juice

1 tablespoon cornstarch mixed with 1 tablespoon of water

Directions:

In a large pot add 2 tablespoons of vegetable oil. Saute onions, celery, and carrots. Sprinkle the vegetables with a pinch of salt to help them release the water in the vegetables. When the onions begin to become translucent add bell pepper and garlic. Continue to saute vegetables until the garlic becomes fragrant. If using canned black beans rinse to remove excess starch. Add beans and vegetable stock to pot. Add 1 teaspoon of salt and the cumin to the soup. Allow the soup to simmer for about 10 minutes to heat through. Taste soup, and adjust salt if needed. Add cornstarch and water mixture to the soup. It will help thicken the soup. Just before serving, add the lemon juice.

Nutrition:

Calories 192

Total fat 4 g

Saturated fat 3 g

Carbs 30 g

Sugar 2 g

Fiber 10 g

Protein 9 g

Sodium 466 mg

Appetizers

White Spinach Queso

Try our white spinach queso with Pico de Gallo salsa, Queso fresco crumbles and Guacamole.

Preparation Time: 5 minutes

Cooking Time: 10 minutes

Servings: 12

Ingredients:

2 tablespoons flour

8 ounces white American cheese

2 cups baby spinach leaves, fresh

¾ cup whole milk

2 tablespoons butter

½ teaspoon garlic powder

2 cups Jack cheese

1 tablespoon canola oil

Optional Ingredients:

Queso fresco crumbles

Pico de Gallo salsa

Guacamole

Directions:

Set your oven to broil. Now, over medium high heat in a large, cast iron skillet; heat the canola oil until hot. Add and cook the spinach until just wilted; immediately remove from the hot pan. Add butter to the hot pan and then add the flour, stir well & cook for a few seconds then slowly add the milk.

Add in the garlic powder; whisk well then add the cheeses. Continue to stir the mixture until thick & bubbly, for a minute or two and then, add in the spinach leaves; stir well.

Broil until the top turn golden brown, for a couple of minutes. Top with salsa, guacamole and queso; serve immediately & enjoy.

Nutrition:

Calories: 459

Fat: 15 g

Carbohydrates: 67 g

Protein: 15 g

Sodium: 1008 mg

Awesome Blossom Petals

Awesome blossom petals is a perfect time to enjoy without other commitment, just you and the blossom petals in your hands. Best for movie night snack!

Preparation Time: 15 minutes

Cooking Time: 15 minutes

Servings: 6

Ingredients:

For Seasoned Breading:

¼ teaspoon onion powder

2 ½ cups flour

½ teaspoon ground black pepper

2 teaspoons seasoned salt

½ teaspoon paprika

1 cup buttermilk

¼ teaspoon garlic powder

For Blossom Sauce:

1/8 teaspoon cayenne pepper

2 tablespoons ketchup

½ cup sour cream

1 ½ teaspoons prepared horseradish

½ teaspoon seasoned salt

Other ingredients

Vegetable oil for frying

Directions:

For Blossom Sauce:

Combine the sour cream with ketchup, horseradish, cayenne pepper and seasoned salt in a small bowl; stir the ingredients well. Cover & let chill in a refrigerator until ready to serve.

For Onion:

Peel the onion.

Cut the stem of the onion off; place it on the cutting board, stem side down. Cut the onion horizontally and vertically into half then make two more diagonal cuts.

For Breading:

Add buttermilk in a large bowl.

Combine flour together with garlic powder, black pepper, paprika, onion powder and seasoned salt in a separate bowl. Using a large fork; give the ingredients a good stir until well mixed.

Put the onions first into the flour and then dip them into the buttermilk; then into the flour again. Let the onions to rest on the wire rack.

For Cooking:

Preheat oil until it reaches 350 F. Work in batches & add the onions into the hot oil (ensure that you don't overcrowd the onions); cook until turn golden brown, for 2 to 3 minutes.

Remove them from the hot oil & then place them on a wire rack to drain.

Serve hot & enjoy.

Nutrition:

Calories: 158

Fat: 5 g

Carbohydrates: 20 g

Protein:17 g

Olive Garden Paste e Fagioli

Pasta e Fagioli is a famous soup for rainy days with grated fresh parmesan cheese.

Preparation Time: 10 minutes

Cooking Time: 25 minutes

Servings: 8

Ingredients:

1 tablespoon of olive oil

1 lb. ground of sausage

2/3 cup of diced carrots

2/3 cup cut celery

2/3 cup white or yellow onion

4 garlic, chopped

1 can of dry great Northern beans

1 can red kidney beans, drained

1 cup drained ditalini pasta

2 boxes Chicken Broth

2 cans Organic Diced Tomatoes

¼ cup grated fresh Parmesan cheese

1 tablespoon fresh chopped parsley

Salt and pepper, to taste

Directions:

In a huge pot, heat olive oil over medium-high warmth. At the point when oil is hot, include hotdog, carrots, celery, onion and garlic to pot and cook, mixing once, until frankfurter is cooked through and onion and garlic have relaxed and get fragrant.

Include beans, pasta, stock and tomatoes. Mix until all around blended. Spread and cook for 15 minutes, or until pasta is still somewhat firm.

Salt and pepper to taste. Serve beat with Parmesan and new parsley

Nutrition:

Calories: 345

Fat: 14 g

Carbohydrates: 34 g

Protein: 54 g

Sodium: 1435 mg

Texas Chili Fries

Crispy chili fries topped with 1 bag cheese blend and packed up with crispy bacon and jalapenos.

Preparation Time: 10 minutes

Cooking Time: 20 minutes

Servings: 4

Ingredients:

1 package of bacon

1 bag cheese blend, shredded

Ranch salad dressing

1 bag steak fries, frozen

1 jar jalapeno peppers

Directions:

Evenly spread the fries over a large-sized cookie sheet & bake as per the directions mentioned on the package.

Line strips of bacon on a separate cookie sheet & bake until crispy.

When the bacon and fries are done; remove them from the oven.

Add a thick layer of jalapenos and cheese; crumble the bacon over the fries.

Bake in the oven again until the cheese is completely melted.

Serve hot with some Ranch salad dressing on side and enjoy.

Nutrition:

Calories: 537

Fat: 17 g

Carbohydrates: 56 g

Protein: 36 g

Sodium: 683 mg

Raspberry Lemonade

The Raspberry Lemonade is completely sweet and tasty. Only 2 minutes to prepare and 3 minutes to cook.

Preparation Time: 2 minutes

Cooking Time: 3 minutes

Servings: 8

Ingredients:

1 cup water

1 cup sugar

1 cup freshly squeezed lemon juice

1 ½ cups fresh

Directions:

In a pan, heat the water with sugar well until the sugar completely dissolves.

Meanwhile, purée the raspberries in a blender. Add the contents of the saucepan and the cup of lemon juice.

Wet the rim of your glass and dip it into a bit of sugar to coat the rim before pouring the lemonade into the glass.

Nutrition:

Calories: 234

Fat: 56. 2 g

Carbohydrates: 23. 8 g

Protein: 23. 5 g

Sodium: 1324 mg

Panda Express's Cream Cheese Rangoon

Panda Express's Cream Cheese Rangoon are your perfect appetizer made with a creamy main and crispy wrapper.

Preparation Time: 5 minutes

Cooking Time: 5 minutes

Servings: 24 minutes

Ingredients:

¼ cup green onions, chopped

½ pound cream cheese, softened

½ teaspoon garlic powder

½ teaspoon salt

24 wonton wrappers

Oil for frying

Directions:

Add the green onions, cream cheese, garlic powder and salt to a medium sized bowl and mix together.

Lay the wonton wrappers out and moisten the edges of the first one. Add about ½ tablespoon of filling to the center of the wrapper and seal by pinching the edges together, starting with the corners and working your way inward. Make sure it is sealed tightly. Repeat with the remaining wrappers.

Add about 3 inches of oil to a large pot. Heat it to about 350°F, then add the wontons a few at a time and cook until brown.

Remove from oil and place on a paper-towel-lined plate to drain.

Nutrition:

Calories: 193

Fat: 5 g

Carbohydrates: 100 g

Protein: 11 g

Sodium: 123 g

PF Chang's Hot and Sour Soup

A hot and sour soup is best for quick dinner recipe. Make yours at home and you won't be disappointed.

Preparation Time: 10 minutes

Cooking Time: 10 minutes

Servings: 4-6

Ingredients:

6 ounces chicken breasts, cut into thin strips

1-quart chicken stock

1 cup soy sauce

1 teaspoon white pepper

1 (6 ounce) can bamboo shoots, cut into strips

6 ounces wood ear mushrooms, cut into strips or canned straw mushrooms, if wood ear can't be found

½ cup cornstarch

½ cup water

2 eggs, beaten

½ cup white vinegar

6 ounces silken tofu, cut into strips

Sliced green onions for garnish

Directions:

In a nourishment processor or blender, finely mince ½ pound of the shrimp. Dice the other ½ pound of shrimp. In a blending bowl, combine both the minced and diced shrimp with the remaining fixings. Spoon around 1 teaspoon of the blend into each wonton wrapper. Damp the edges of the wrapper together with your finger, at that point overlap up and seal firmly. Cover and refrigerate for at slightest an hour. In a medium bowl, combine all of the fixings for the sauce and mix until well combined. When prepared to serve, bubble water in a saucepan and cover with a steamer. You will need to gently oil the steamer to keep the dumplings from staying. Steam the dumplings for 7–10 minutes. Serve with sauce.

Nutrition:

Calories: 345

Fat: 1.2 g

Carbohydrates: 2.2 g

Protein: 23.3 g

Sodium: 145

Kids Recipes

Miso-Grilled Shrimp Skewers

Miso-grilled shrimp skewers is a fresh and tasty recipe made on the grill in just 7 minutes. It is a recipe for a short time and nutritious dinner.

Preparation Time: 20 minutes

Cooking Time: 7 minutes

Servings: 3

Ingredients:

2 tablespoons freshly squeezed lime juice, with extra wedges for garnish

2 tablespoons mirin

2 tablespoons yellow miso

1 tablespoon sesame oil

1 tablespoon fresh ginger, peeled and finely grated

1 large garlic clove, finely grated

1pound large shrimp, shelled and

Chopped scallions

Sunflower sprouts

Green beans, steamed and crunchy

Sliced English or Persian cucumbers

Salad greens

Fresh cilantro leaves

Cooked rice or steamed buns

Directions:

Make the glaze. In a large bowl, whisk together the lime juice, mirin, miso, sesame oil, ginger, and garlic. Add the shrimp, and toss to coat. Let marinate for 20 minutes.

Grill the shrimp. Preheat a grill pan over medium-high heat. Thread the shrimp onto metal skewers, piercing the shrimp at the tail end and at the thickest part of the body to secure. Grill the shrimp over medium-high heat until lightly charred and opaque, turning once, about 5 minutes.

Serve. These glazed and grilled shrimps are great served in steamed buns with chopped fresh scallions and cilantro, over rice, or alongside crunchy green beans, greens, or Asian Cucumber Salad

Nutrition:

Calories 174,

Fat 9g,

Fiber 2g,

Carbs 28g

Protein 7g

Pizza Party

Serve a DIY delicious pizza party recipe for kids with mushrooms, black olives and a handful fresh basil.

Preparation Time: 20 minutes

Cooking Time: 10 minutes

Serves: 8

Ingredients

1 bell pepper (optional)

4 mushrooms (optional)

1 handful fresh basil

1 cup water, heated to 110°F

1 tablespoon sugar

1 tablespoon olive oil, plus 2 teaspoons for coating the pans

2¼ teaspoons instant yeast

2¾ cups whole-wheat flour or white whole-wheat flour, plus more for dusting the work area

1 teaspoon salt

1 cup pizza sauce

2 cups shredded mozzarella cheese

¼ cup sliced black olives (optional)

Directions

Preheat the oven, and cut the veggies. With a rack in the top half of the oven, preheat the oven to 500°F. Using a cutting board and a kid-safe knife, cut the bell pepper (if using) in half. Scoop out the seeds and cut the bell pepper into strips. Cut the mushrooms (if using) into small cubes. Tear the basil into small pieces with your hands.

Mix the dough ingredients. Use the cooking thermometer to check the water temperature. In a small bowl, whisk (Use a whisk or fork to stir ingredients) the warm water, sugar, oil, and yeast. Let it sit for 5 minutes. In a food processor, combine the flour and salt. Pulse (Press and release the pulse button on the food processor or blender to get a short burst of mixing) for 20 seconds, until combined. Slowly pour the water-yeast mixture into the food processor, and pulse until a ball forms, about 1 minute.

Knead and roll out the dough. Spread about 1 tablespoon of flour onto a clean surface. Remove the dough from the unplugged food processor, and place it on the floured surface. Knead (Use hands to press and fold dough to help it combine and eventually rise) it until it comes together, about 2 minutes. Divide the dough in half, and use a rolling pin to roll the dough into two circles. Use the ruler to measure them to about 10 inches across. Rub about 1 teaspoon of olive oil onto a round baking pan to lightly coat it (use more oil if needed). Use both hands to lift the dough into the baking pan. Repeat with the second dough round, the remaining teaspoon of oil, and the other round baking pan.

Top the pizzas and bake. Spread the pizza sauce onto the two rounds of dough. Top with the cheese, cut vegetables, basil, and olives (if using). Bake on the top rack for about 12 minutes, until the crust and cheese are slightly golden. Let cool. Use a pizza cutter to slice the pizza and serve

Nutrition

Calories 250

Fats 18.44g

Carbs 1.59g

Net Carbs 1.49g

Protein 18.58g

Crunchy Deviled Chicken

Kids loves fried chicken. Why not try this crunchy deviled chicken at home for your little kids. It's easy to make.

Preparation Time: 10 minutes

Cooking Time: 20 minutes

Serves: 4

Ingredients

1¼ cups panko bread crumbs

3 tablespoons spicy brown mustard

1 large egg

½ teaspoon smoked paprika

1¼ pounds skinless, boneless chicken thighs

1pound medium carrots, halved lengthwise

½ teaspoon salt

Salad greens

Directions

Preparing the Ingredients

Preheat oven to 450°F. Spray 2 rimmed baking sheets with nonstick cooking spray.

On medium plate, spread panko. In shallow bowl with wire whisk, combine mustard, egg, and paprika until blended.

Dip chicken in egg mixture. Coat with panko, firmly pressing to adhere. Place on 1 prepared baking sheet. On other prepared baking sheet, arrange carrots.

Bake

Spray chicken and carrots with nonstick cooking spray; sprinkle with salt. Bake for 20 minutes or until carrots are tender and chicken is no longer pink throughout. Serve over salad greens.

Nutrition

Calories: About 355,

Protein: 30G,

Carbohydrates: 31G,

Total Fat: 10G

(Saturated Fat: 3G),

Fiber: 4G,

Sodium: 605MG

Triple-Decker Tortilla Pie

This tortilla pie is a triple decker quesadilla filled with rotisserie chicken and overload cheese. It's a perfect dinner recipe for your kids.

Preparation Time: 20 minutes

Cooking Time: 10 minutes

Serves: 4

Ingredients

1 (2-to 2½-pound) rotisserie chicken

1 can (12 ounces) enchilada sauce

3 burrito-size flour tortillas

4 ounces shredded Monterey Jack cheese (½ cup)

Shredded romaine lettuce, halved cherry tomatoes, and diced avocado, for garnish

Directions

1 Preparing the Ingredients. Preheat oven to 450°F.

Remove skin and bones from chicken; shred meat. In medium bowl, combine chicken and enchilada sauce. Place 1 flour tortilla in 10-to 12-inch skillet. Top with half of chicken mixture and ⅓ cup Monterey Jack cheese. Repeat with 1 tortilla, remaining chicken mixture, and ⅓ cup cheese. Top with remaining tortilla and remaining ⅓ cup cheese.

2 Bake. Bake for 8 to 10 minutes or until heated through and cheese has melted. Garnish with lettuce, tomatoes, and avocado.

Nutrients:

Calories: 550

Protein: 48G

Carbohydrates: 33G

Total Fat: 24G

(Saturated Fat: 9G)

Fiber: 2G,

Sodium: 980MG

Fish and Chips

A super easy recipe to make at home for your kids with potato chips and 2 dipping sauce for the fish and chips.

Preparation Time: 20 minutes

Cooking Time: 10 minutes

Serves: 4

Ingredients

1 bag (6 ounces) salt-and-vinegar potato chips, finely crushed

3 large egg whites

1½ pounds cod fillets, cut into strips

½ teaspoon salt

1pound frozen peas

3 tablespoons butter

1 tablespoon fresh lemon juice

¼ teaspoon ground black pepper

Lemon wedges and snipped fresh chives, for garnish

Directions

1 Preparing the Ingredients. Preheat oven to 450°F. Line large baking sheet with foil; spray generously with nonstick spray. On medium plate, spread potato chips. In pie plate with fork, beat egg whites. Working in batches, dip cod in egg. Coat with potato chips, firmly pressing so potato chips stick to egg. Arrange cod on prepared pan; spray with nonstick cooking spray.

2 Bake. Bake for 12 minutes or until cod is white throughout. Sprinkle with ¼ teaspoon salt. Meanwhile, in large microwave-safe bowl, combine peas, butter, lemon juice, remaining ¼ teaspoon salt, and pepper. Cover with vented microwave-safe plastic wrap, microwave on High for 5 minutes or until hot. In food processor with knife blade attached, pulse pea mixture until smooth.

Serve cod with peas; garnish with lemon wedges and chives.

Nutrition

Calories: About 480,

Protein: 30G,

Carbohydrates: 58G

Total Fat: 15G, (Saturated Fat: 5G),

Fiber: 5G,

Sodium: 705MG

Garlic-Shrimp Caesar Salad

Get this Garlic-shrimp Caesar salad recipe here with fresh lettuce, sliced radicchio and croutons for a healthy meal. A resourceful and beautiful meal for your kids.

Preparation Time: 10 minutes

Cooking Time: 20 minutes

Serves: 4

Ingredients

1pound peeled and deveined medium

Shrimp

2 tablespoons olive oil

4 tablespoons fresh lemon juice

4 garlic cloves

2 teaspoons Dijon mustard

1 teaspoon paprika

¼ cup plain nonfat Greek yogurt

3 tablespoons grated Parmesan cheese

¼ teaspoon salt

¼ teaspoon ground black pepper

1 head romaine lettuce

1 heart radicchio, sliced

1 cup croutons

Directions

Preparing the Ingredients. Preheat oven to 400°F. Line large cookie sheet with foil.

In large bowl, combine shrimp, oil, 1 tablespoon lemon juice, 3 garlic cloves crushed through press, mustard, and paprika, tossing to coat. Refrigerate for 10 minutes.

Meanwhile, in large serving bowl, with wire whisk, mix yogurt, remaining 3 tablespoons lemon juice, Parmesan, remaining garlic clove crushed through press, salt, and pepper until blended. Spread shrimp on prepared cookie sheet. Roast for 10 minutes or until pink.

Add chopped romaine and radicchio to serving bowl; toss to coat with dressing. Top with shrimp and croutons.

Nutrition

Calories: About 240,

Protein: 22G,

Carbohydrates: 17G,

Total Fat: 10G (Saturated Fat: 2G),

Fiber: 4G,

Sodium: 910MG

Hoisin-Glazed Salmon

This simple hoisin-glazed salmon is ideal for those who are not load up their lunches. A sweet and delicious recipe whether warm or cold. If you want a finest seafood then try this one at home.

Preparation Time: 10 minutes

Cooking Time: 25 minutes

Serves: 4

Ingredients

4 salmon fillets (6 ounces each), skin removed

1 tablespoon hoisin sauce

Crushed red pepper (optional)

1½ pounds cauliflower florets

1 tablespoon vegetable oil

¼ teaspoon salt

¼ cup chopped peanuts

¼ cup chopped fresh cilantro

Directions

Preparing the Ingredients. Preheat oven to 425°F. Tear four (18-by-12-inch) sheets of foil. For each packet, place 1 piece foil on cutting board with longer side of foil facing you. Place 1 salmon fillet in center of each. Brush each fillet with 1 tablespoon hoisin sauce and sprinkle with pinch of crushed red pepper, if using. In large bowl, combine cauliflower, oil, and salt, tossing to coat. Arrange cauliflower around each fillet. Fold foil around salmon and vegetables; tightly crimp the edges to form total of 4 packets.

Bake. Place packets on large cookie sheet. Bake for 15 minutes or until cauliflower is tender. Open packets carefully, allowing steam to escape. Garnish with peanuts and cilantro.

Nutrition

Calories: About 480,

Protein: 30G,

Carbohydrates: 58G

Total Fat: 15G, (Saturated Fat: 5G),

Fiber: 5G,

Sodium: 705MG

Easiest-Ever Spinach Lasagna

This spinach lasagna recipe is the easiest lasagna ever to serve to your kids. It is a perfect recipe for lunch or dinner to satisfy your cravings.

Preparation Time: 10 minutes

Cooking Time: 4 hours

Serves: 8

Ingredients

1 container (15 ounces) part-skim ricotta

Cheese

1 package (10 ounces) frozen chopped

Spinach, thawed and squeezed dry

8 ounces shredded mozzarella cheese

1 large egg, lightly beaten

¼ teaspoon salt

1 jar (32 ounces) marinara sauce

1 box (9 ounces) no-boil lasagna noodles

Directions

Preparing the Ingredients. In large bowl, combine ricotta, spinach, 1 cup mozzarella, egg, and salt. Spray a 6-to 6½-quart slow-cooker bowl with nonstick cooking spray. In bowl, alternately layer marinara sauce, noodles, and ricotta mixture, starting and ending with marinara sauce and breaking noodles to fit. Top with remaining 1 cup mozzarella.

Cover slow cooker with lid and cook as manufacturer directs on low for 4 hours or until noodles are tender.

Nutrients:

Calories: 230

Sodium 189mg

Carbohydrates 13.7g

Fat 7.7g

Protein 7.6g

Tomato Soup Mac and Cheese

Tomato soup mac and cheese is a perfect and traditional combination of grilled cheese. This easy cavatappi pasta is exactly what your family will love.

Preparation Time: 20 minutes

Cooking Time: 1 hour

Serves: 8

Ingredients:

1pound cavatappi pasta

4 tablespoons unsalted butter

¼ cup all-purpose flour

2½ cups whole milk

¼ teaspoon salt

1pound American cheese, chopped

1½ cups marinara sauce

2 tablespoons tomato paste

2 tablespoons plain dried bread crumbs

Directions

Preparing the Ingredients. Preheat oven to 375°F. Line rimmed baking sheet with foil.

Heat large covered saucepot of water to boiling over high heat. Add cavatappi; cook for 5 minutes. Drain well. Meanwhile, in 5- to 6-quart saucepot, melt butter over medium heat. Sprinkle flour over butter. Cook for 1 minute, stirring. Slowly whisk in milk until smooth. Add salt. Heat to boiling over high heat, whisking often. Reduce heat to medium. Simmer for 2 minutes or until slightly thickened, stirring occasionally.

Reduce heat to medium-low. Gradually stir in cheese by handful until smooth, letting cheese melt before adding next batch. Whisk in marinara sauce and tomato paste. Add cavatappi; toss to coat well. Place ramekins on prepared pan. Transfer mixture to eight (8-ounce) ramekins; top with bread crumbs. Spray crumbs with nonstick cooking spray.

Bake. Bake for 30 to 35 minutes or until sauce is bubbling and crumbs are golden.

Nutrients:

Calories: 115

Sodium 129mg

Carbohydrates 8.6g

Fat 7.7g

Protein 4.4g

Corkscrews with Cheese, Tomatoes & Peas

Have the kids enjoy eating this corkscrews with cheese, tomatoes and peas after cooking.

Preparation Time: 10 minutes

Cooking Time: 10 minutes

Serves: 8

Ingredients

12 ounces cavatappi pasta

1 package (10 ounces) frozen peas

1 tablespoon butter

2 tablespoons all-purpose flour

¼ teaspoon salt

¼ teaspoon ground black pepper

2 cups low-fat (2%) milk

4 ounces extra-sharp cheddar cheese, shredded (½ cup)

½ cup grated pecorino cheese plus additional for serving

2 medium tomatoes, chopped

2 tablespoons snipped fresh chives

Directions

Preparing the Ingredients. Heat large covered saucepot of salted water to boiling over high heat. Add cavatappi and cook as label directs, adding peas to saucepot for 1 minute before pasta is done. Meanwhile, in 4-quart saucepan, melt butter over medium heat. With wire whisk, stir in flour, salt, and pepper until smooth. Cook for 1 minute, stirring constantly. Gradually whisk in milk; heat to boiling over medium-high heat, stirring constantly. Boil for 1 minute. Remove saucepan from heat; stir in cheddar and ½ cup pecorino until smooth.

Drain pasta and peas well; stir into saucepan with cheese mixture until coated. Top with tomatoes and chives. Serve with pecorino.

Nutrition

Calories: About 480,

Protein: 30G,

Carbohydrates: 58G

Total Fat: 15G, (Saturated Fat: 5G),

Fiber: 5G,

Sodium: 705MG

Cheesy Hassel backs

Easy cheesy classic baked potato filled with bacon and cheddar cheese. A recipes that full of flavor and nice texture. Bake some potatoes and try this delicious recipe for your kids.

Preparation Time: 15 minutes

Cooking Time: 40 minutes

Serves: 6

Ingredients

6 medium russet potatoes

3 tablespoons olive oil

¾ teaspoon salt

4 ounces cheddar cheese, cut into thin sticks

Directions

Preparing the Ingredients

Preheat oven to 425°F. Thinly slice potatoes (but don't cut all the way through). Arrange on rimmed baking sheet. Brush tops with 1½ tablespoons oil.

Bake. Bake for 30 minutes. Brush tops with remaining 1½ tablespoons oil; sprinkle with salt. Bake for 30 minutes or until tender. Remove potatoes from oven; carefully place cheddar sticks between slices. Bake for 5 minutes longer or until cheese melts

Nutrition

Calories: About 305,

Protein: 8G,

Carbohydrates: 39G,

Total Fat: 13G (Saturated Fat: 4G),

Fiber: 2G,

Sodium: 424MG

Frosted Lemonade

Easy cheesy classic baked potato filled with bacon and cheddar cheese. A recipes that full of flavor and nice texture. Bake some potatoes and try this delicious recipe for your kids.

Preparation Time: 10 minutes

Cooking Time: 0 minutes

Serves: 3

Ingredients

1/2 c. freshly squeezed lemon juice

1/2 c. sugar

2 c. water

6 c. vanilla ice cream

sliced lemons, for garnish

Directions

Mix lemon juice and sugar together in a pitcher until the sugar is fully dissolved. Add water to dilute and chill.

Into a blender, add lemonade and ice cream. Blend until smooth and divide among 3 cups. Garnish with slices of lemon and serve.

Nutrition

Calories: About 305

Protein: 8G,

Carbohydrates: 39G,

Fiber: 2G,

Sodium: 424MG

Gluten Free Recipes

Mediterranean Trout With Sautéed Vegetables

This Mediterranean trout with sauteed vegetables is a perfect way to serve for dinner. It will give you a great dinner. Try this lovely recipe at your home.

Preparation Time: 10 minutes

Cooking Time: 20 minutes

Servings: 4

Ingredients:

2 pounds (907 g) rainbow trout fillets

Salt and ground white pepper, to taste

1 tablespoon olive oil

1-pound (454 g) asparagus

4 medium golden potatoes, thinly sliced

1 garlic clove, finely minced

1 scallion, thinly sliced, green and white parts separated

2 Roma tomatoes, chopped

1 large carrot, thinly sliced

8 pitted kalamata olives, chopped

¼ cup ground cumin

2 tablespoons paprika

2 tablespoons dried parsley

1 tablespoon vegetable bouillon seasoning

½ cup dry white wine

Directions:

In a bowl, rub the rainbow trout fillets with salt and white pepper. Set aside.

Heat the olive oil in a large skillet over medium heat. Sauté the asparagus, golden potatoes, garlic, and the white parts of the scallion in the oil for about 5 minutes, stirring occasionally, or until the garlic is fragrant.

Toss in the tomatoes, carrot slices and olives, then continue to cook until the vegetables are tender but still crisp, about 5 to 7 minutes.

Add the cumin, paprika, parsley, vegetable bouillon seasoning, and salt. Stir to combine well. Top with the seasoned fillets and slowly pour in the white wine.

Turn the heat down to low, cover, and bring to a simmer for about 6 minutes, or until the flesh is opaque and it flakes apart easily.

Remove from the heat and sprinkle the scallion greens on top for garnish before serving.

TIP: If you don't want to cook the whole trout fillets at a time, you can cut them into uniform pieces and cover with plastic wrap, then put in the freezer for next meal.

Nutrition:

Calories 495

Carbohydrates 41.2g

Protein 40.2g

Fat 19.3g

Sodium 732mg

Cholesterol 110mg

Garlicky Branzino With Fresh Herbs

Are looking for delightful and delicious recipe? This one is good for you!

Preparation Time: 10 minutes

Cooking Time: 20 minutes

Servings: 2

Ingredients:

1½ pounds (680 g) branzino, scaled and gutted

Salt and freshly ground black pepper, to taste

1 tablespoon olive oil

1 sliced lemon

3 minced garlic cloves

¼ cup chopped fresh herbs (any mixture of thyme, oregano, rosemary, and parsley)

Directions:

Preheat the oven to 425°F (220°C).

Arrange the branzino on a baking dish. Using a sharp knife, make 4 slits in the fish, about 1½ inches apart.

Generously brush the fish inside and out with salt and pepper, then drizzle with 1 tablespoon olive oil.

Place the lemon slices, garlic gloves, and fresh herbs into the cavity of the fish.

Roast the fish in the preheated oven for 15 to 20 minutes, or until the fish flakes easily with a fork and juices run clear.

Allow to cool for 5 minutes and remove the lemon slices before serving.

TIP: To make this a complete meal, serve it with sautéed mushroom and green beans as a side dish.

Nutrition:

Calories 290

Carbohydrates: 2.2g

Protein 42.3g

Fat: 12.3g

Sodium 150mg

Cholesterol 92mg

Shrimp With Black Bean Pasta

When your tummy is hungry and you want something delicious to eat, try this shrimp with black bean pasta to fill hungry tummy.

Preparation Time: 10 minutes

Cooking Time: 15 minutes

Servings: 4

Ingredients:

1 package black bean pasta

4 tablespoons olive oil

3 garlic cloves, minced

1 onion, finely chopped

1 pound (454 g) fresh shrimp, peeled and deveined

Salt and pepper, to taste

¾ cup low-sodium chicken broth

¼ cup basil, cut into strips

Directions:

Put the black bean pasta in a large pot of boiling water and cook for 6 minutes.

Remove the pasta from the heat. Drain and rinse with cold water, then set the pasta aside on a platter.

Heat the olive oil in a large skillet over medium heat. Add the garlic and onion, then cook for 3 minutes until the onion is translucent.

Add the shrimp and season with salt and pepper. Cook for 3 minutes, stirring occasionally, or until the shrimp is opaque. Pour in the chicken broth and let it simmer for 2 to 3 minutes until heated through.

Remove the shrimp from the heat to the platter of pasta. Pour the liquid over the pasta and garnish with basil, then serve.

TIP: If the black bean pasta is not available, you can try any of your favorite pasta with this recipe. And for a unique twist, the jumbo lump crab meat can be substituted for shrimp.

Nutrition:

Calories 670

Carbohydrates 73.3g

Protein 57.2g

Fat: 19.2g

Cholesterol 225mg

Sodium 610mg

Spanish Style Salmon With Vegetables

Here's one of the best recipe that you will never get tired of eating when you taste it. Spanish style salmon with vegetables is really perfect for you.

Preparation Time: 10 minutes

Cooking Time: 20 minutes

Servings: 4

Ingredients:

2 small red onions, thinly sliced

1 cup shaved fennel bulbs

1 cup cherry tomatoes

15 green pimiento-stuffed olives

1 teaspoon cumin seeds

½ teaspoon smoked paprika

Salt and freshly ground black pepper, to taste

4 (8-ounce / 227-g) salmon fillets

½ cup chicken broth, low-sodium

2 to 4 tablespoons olive oil

2 cups cooked couscous

Directions:

Preheat the oven to 375°F (190°C).

Arrange the red onions, fennel bulbs, cherry tomatoes, and olives on two baking sheets. Sprinkle with cumin seeds, paprika, salt, and pepper.

Place the salmon fillets on top of the vegetables and sprinkle with salt. Pour the chicken broth evenly over the two baking sheets and drizzle with olive oil.

Bake in the preheated oven for 18 to 20 minutes until the vegetables are tender and the fish is flaky, checking regularly to ensure they don't overcook.

Divide the cooked couscous among four serving plates and top with vegetables and fillets, then serve.

TIP: If you can't find the salmon fillets, you can use other fish of your choice, like swordfish. The leftovers can be stored for salmon patties.

Nutrition:

Calories 480

Carbohydrates: : 26.2g

Protein: 50.2g

Fat 18.3g

Sodium 295mg

Cholesterol 168mg

Swordfish With Lemon And Tarragon

A combination of pasta, tomato and squash gives colorful light in this recipes. Delicious and flavor dish meal for your visitors.

Preparation Time: 5 minutes

Cooking Time: 15 minutes

Servings: 4

Ingredients:

1-pound (454 g) swordfish steaks, cut into 2-inch pieces

1 teaspoon salt, or more to taste

¼ teaspoon freshly ground black pepper

¼ cup olive oil and plus 2 tablespoons, divided

2 tablespoons unsalted butter

2 tablespoons fresh tarragon, chopped

Zest and juice of 1 lemon

Zest and juice of 2 clementine

Directions:

Season the swordfish steaks with salt and pepper in a bowl.

Heat ¼ cup olive oil in a large skillet over medium-high heat.

Sear the swordfish steaks for 2 to 3 minutes per side until lightly browned.

With a slotted spoon, remove the swordfish steaks from the heat to a plate.

Add 2 tablespoons olive oil and butter to the skillet over medium-low heat.

When the butter melts, fold in the tarragon, lemon and clementine zests and juices. Season with salt and stir well.

Return the swordfish steaks to the skillet. Cook for about 2 minutes more and let the swordfish steaks coat in the sauce thoroughly.

Remove from the heat and serve on plates.

TIP: You can try fresh sea scallops with this recipe and it tastes great paired with riced cauliflower or sautéed greens.

Nutrition:

Calories383

Carbohydrates 3.2g

Protein: 23.2g

Fat: 31.2g

Sodium 3726mg

Stuffed Squid With Spinach And Cheese

A comforting squid dish with spinach and cheese for your

cravings!

Preparation Time: 15 minutes

Cooking Time: 30 minutes

Servings: 4

Ingredients:

4 tablespoons olive oil, divided

FILLING:

¼ cup olive oil

8 ounces (227 g) frozen spinach, thawed and drained

¼ cup sun-dried tomatoes, chopped

½ cup chopped pitted olives

4 ounces (113 g) goat cheese, crumbled

2 garlic cloves, finely minced

¼ cup fresh flat-leaf Italian parsley, chopped

¼ teaspoon freshly ground black pepper

2 pounds (907 g) baby squid, cleaned and tentacles removed

Directions:

Preheat the oven to 350°F (180°C). Coat the bottom of a baking dish with 2 tablespoons olive oil and set aside.

Make the filling: Mix together ¼ cup olive oil, spinach, tomatoes, olives, goat cheese, garlic, parsley, and pepper in a bowl until well combined.

On a clean work surface, spoon 2 tablespoons of the filling onto each baby squid, then arrange them on the prepared baking dish. Evenly pour the remaining olive oil over the squid.

Bake in the preheated oven for 25 to 30 minutes until cooked through.

Remove from the oven and cool for 8 minutes before serving.

TIP: If you can't find the baby squid, you can replace it with calamari steaks, but don't remember to increase the cook time.

Nutrition:

Calories 473

Carbohydrates: 7.3g

Protein: 24.3g

Fat: 37.4g

Cholesterol 8mg

Sodium 578mg

Mediterranean Sheet Pan Fish Fillets

A simple and healthy dinner recipe brings the flavor to your home and only 10 minutes cook.

Preparation Time: 10 minutes

Cooking Time: 10 minutes

Servings: 4

Ingredients:

4 (4-ounce/ 113-g) fish fillets, such as cod or tilapia (½ inch thick)

2 tablespoons olive oil

1 tablespoon balsamic vinegar

2½ cups (about 12 ounces) green beans

1 pint (about 2 cups) cherry or grape tomatoes

Nonstick cooking spray

Directions:

Preheat the oven to 400°F (205°C). Spray two large baking sheets with nonstick cooking spray.

Arrange two fish fillets on each baking sheet and set aside.

Stir together the olive oil and vinegar in a bowl.

In a separate bowl, mix the green beans and tomatoes. Pour the olive oil and vinegar mixture into the bowl of vegetables. Toss gently to coat the vegetables in the mixture.

Divide the coated vegetables among the fish fillets and pour over the mixture.

Bake in the preheated oven for 5 to 8 minutes, or until the flesh is opaque and it flakes apart easily.

Allow to cool for 5 minutes and serve hot.

TIP: For additional zest, you can add a sprinkle of lemon juice and chopped parsley. You also can serve it with sautéed zucchini.

Enjoy!

Nutrition:

Calories 245

Carbohydrates 57mg

Protein: 22.1g

Fat: 14.3g

Cholesterol 189mg

Sodium 135mg

Quick Mussels With White Wine Sauce

Mussels with white wine sauce is an easy one pot meal with simple ingredients. This mussels recipe suits for your appetizer.

Preparation Time: 5 minutes

Cooking Time: 10 minutes

Servings: 4

Ingredients:

2 pounds (907 g) small mussels

1 tablespoon olive oil

3 garlic cloves, sliced

1 cup thinly sliced red onion (about ½ medium onion)

2 (¼-inch-thick) lemon slices

1 cup dry white wine

¼ teaspoon kosher or sea salt

¼ teaspoon freshly ground black pepper

Fresh lemon wedges, for garnish

Directions:

Put the small mussels in a colander in the sink and run them under cold water. Discard the open shells or damaged shells. Set the mussels aside in the colander.

In a large skillet, heat the olive oil over medium-high heat. Add the garlic and onion, cook for 3 to 4 minutes until tender, stirring occasionally.

Add the lemon slices, wine, salt, and pepper. Stir well and allow to simmer for 2 minutes.

Pour in the mussels and cook covered until the mussels open their shells, giving the pan a shake from time to time, about 3 minutes.

With a slotted spoon, transfer the mussels to a serving bowl. Be sure to discard any mussels that are still closed.

Pour the wine sauce over the mussels in the bowl and serve garnished with lemon wedges.

TIP: To make this a complete meal, you can serve it with garlic bread or lemony broth on the side.

Nutrition:

Calories 344

Carbohydrates: 92mg

Protein: 36.4g

Fat: 16.3g

Sodium 1270mg

Desserts

Cherry Chocolate Cobbler

This cherry chocolate cobbler is insanely delicious! Sweet cherry filling is topped with tender chocolate chunk (or chip) biscuits. It is a perfect summer dessert!

Preparation Time: 10 minutes

Cooking Time: 45 minutes

Servings: 8

Ingredients:

1½ cups all-purpose flour

½ cup sugar

2 teaspoons baking powder

½ teaspoon salt

¼ cup butter

6 ounces semisweet chocolate morsels

¼ cup milk

1 egg, beaten

21 ounces cherry pie filling

½ cup finely chopped nuts

Directions:

Preheat the oven to 350°F.

Combine the flour, sugar, baking powder, salt, and butter in a large mixing bowl. Use a pastry blender to cut the mixture until there are lumps the size of small peas.

Melt the chocolate morsels. Let cool for approximately 5 minutes, then add the milk and egg and mix well. Beat into the flour mixture, mixing completely.

Spread the pie filling in a 2-quart casserole dish. Randomly drop the chocolate batter over the filling, then sprinkle with nuts.

Bake for 40–45 minutes.

Serve with a scoop of vanilla ice cream if desired.

Nutrition:

Calories: 510

Sodium 448 mg

Carbohydrates 115g

Fiber 3.1g

Sugar 32g

Protein 6g

Double Fudge Coca-Cola Cake

You can recreate the Double Fudge Coca Cola Cake at home with this easy copycat recipe.

Preparation Time: 15 minutes

Cooking Time: 30 minutes

Servings: 8–10

Ingredients:

1 cup Coca-Cola

½ cup vegetable oil

½ cup (1 stick) salted butter

3 heaping tablespoons dark cocoa powder

2 cups sugar

2 cups all-purpose flour

2 large eggs

½ cup buttermilk

1 teaspoon baking soda

1 teaspoon vanilla extract

Frosting

½ cup (1 stick) salted butter

3 tablespoons dark cocoa powder

6 tablespoons milk

1 teaspoon vanilla extract

4 cups powdered sugar

Directions:

Preheat the oven to 350°F.

Prepare a baking dish by buttering and dusting it with flour.

Combine the sugar and flour in a mixing bowl. Set aside.

Bring the Coca-Cola, oil, butter, and cocoa to a boil in a saucepan. Add the mixture to the mixing bowl and beat on medium for about 1 minute. Add the eggs, buttermilk, baking soda, and vanilla and beat for another 2 minutes or until well mixed.

Pour the batter into the prepared baking pan and bake for 30 minutes or until it passes the toothpick test.

To prepare the frosting, bring the butter, cocoa powder, and milk to a hard simmer. When the mixture is just below boiling, remove from heat and beat in the powdered sugar and vanilla. Pour it over the cake and spread it quickly. Let cool to room temperature, then cover and store in the refrigerator until serving.

Nutrition:

Calories: 790

Sodium 310 mg

Carbohydrates 115g

Fiber 3g

Protein 9g

Chocolate Pecan Pie

Not just any chocolate pie.... this Chocolate Pecan Pie is a cross between a pecan pie, chocolate fudge, molten brownies and a hot fudge chocolate pudding.

Preparation Time: 10 minutes

Cooking Time: 50 minutes

Servings: 8

Ingredients:

3 eggs

½ cup sugar

1 cup corn syrup

½ teaspoon salt

1 teaspoon vanilla extract

¼ cup melted butter

1 cup pecans

3 tablespoons semisweet chocolate chips

1 unbaked pie shell

Directions:

Preheat the oven to 350°F.

Beat together the eggs and sugar in a mixing bowl, then add the corn syrup, salt, vanilla, and butter.

Put the chocolate chips and pecans inside the pie shell and pour the egg mixture over the top.

Bake for 50–60 minutes or until set.

Serve with vanilla ice cream.

Nutrition:

Calories: 560

Sodium 310 mg

Carbohydrates 87g

Fat 33g

Protein 5g

Pumpkin Custard with Gingersnaps

A rich and creamy homemade custard with a ginger snap topping, and a dollop of pumpkin pie spice-infused whipped cream.

Preparation Time: 30 minutes

Cooking Time: 35 minutes

Servings: 8

Ingredients:

Custard

8 egg yolks

1¾ cups (1 15-ounce can) pure pumpkin puree

1¾ cups heavy whipping cream

½ cup sugar

1½ teaspoons pumpkin pie spice

1 teaspoon vanilla

Topping

1 cup crushed gingersnap cookies

1 tablespoon melted butter

Whipped Cream

1 cup heavy whipping cream

1 tablespoon superfine sugar (or regular sugar if you have no caster sugar)

½ teaspoon pumpkin pie spice

Garnish

8 whole gingersnap cookies

Directions:

Preheat the oven to 350°F.

Separate the yolks from 8 eggs and whisk them together in a large mixing bowl until they are well blended and creamy.

Add the pumpkin, sugar, vanilla, heavy cream and pumpkin pie spice and whisk to combine.

Cook the custard mixture in a double boiler, stirring until it has thickened enough that it coats a spoon.

Pour the mixture into individual custard cups or an 8×8-inch baking pan and bake for about 20 minutes if using individual cups or 30–35 minutes for the baking pan, until it is set and a knife inserted comes out clean.

While the custard is baking, make the topping by combining the crushed gingersnaps and melted butter. After the custard has been in the oven for 15 minutes, sprinkle the gingersnap mixture over the top.

When the custard has passed the clean knife test, remove from the oven, and let cool to room temperature.

Whisk the heavy cream and pumpkin pie spice together with the caster sugar and beat just until it thickens.

Serve the custard with the whipped cream and garnish each serving with a gingersnap.

Nutrition:

Calories: 274

Fats 16g

Carbohydrates 26.4g

Fiber 2g

Protein 4.72g

Peach Cobbler

Sweet, ripe peaches and cinnamon-sugar are topped with a flaky pie crust and vanilla bean ice cream

Preparation Time: 10 minutes

Cooking Time: 45 minutes

Servings: 4

Ingredients:

1¼ cups Bisques

1 cup milk

½ cup melted butter

¼ teaspoon nutmeg

½ teaspoon cinnamon

Vanilla ice cream, for serving

Filling

1 (30-ounce) can peaches in syrup, drained

¼ cup sugar

Topping

½ cup brown sugar

¼ cup almond slices

½ teaspoon cinnamon

1 tablespoon melted butter

Directions:

Preheat the oven to 375°F.

Grease the bottom and sides of an 8×8-inch pan.

Whisk together the Bisques, milk, butter, nutmeg, and cinnamon in a large mixing bowl. When thoroughly combined, pour into the greased baking pan.

Mix the peaches and sugar in another mixing bowl. Put the filling on top of the batter in the pan. Bake for about 45 minutes.

In another bowl, mix the brown sugar, almonds, cinnamon, and melted butter. After the cobbler has cooked for 45 minutes, cover evenly with the topping and bake for an additional 10 minutes.

Serve with a scoop of vanilla ice cream.

Nutrition:

Calories: 150

Fats 15g

Carbohydrates 26.4g

Fiber 4g

Protein 6g

Baked Apple Dumplings

Warm, flaky, apple-y sweet and drizzled with a sauce that bakes right with them. These are not difficult to make, just a little time-consuming. Serve warm with whipped cream or ice cream.

Preparation Time: 20 minutes

Cooking Time: 40 minutes

Servings: 2-4

Ingredients:

1 (17½ ounce) package frozen puff pastry, thawed

1 cup sugar

6 tablespoons dry breadcrumbs

2 teaspoons ground cinnamon

1 pinch ground nutmeg

1 egg, beaten

4 Granny Smith apples, peeled, cored and halved

Vanilla ice cream for serving

Icing

1 cup confectioners' sugar

1 teaspoon vanilla extract

3 tablespoons milk

Pecan Streusel

⅔ cup chopped toasted pecans

⅔ cup packed brown sugar

⅔ cup all-purpose flour

5 tablespoons melted butter

Directions:

Preheat the oven to 425°F.

When the puff pastry has completely thawed, roll out each sheet to measure 12 inches by 12 inches. Cut the sheets into quarters. Combine the sugar, breadcrumbs, cinnamon, and nutmeg in a small bowl.

Brush one of the pastry squares with some of the beaten egg. Add about 1 tablespoon of the breadcrumb mixture on top, then add half an apple, core side down, over the crumbs. Add another tablespoon of the breadcrumb mixture.

Seal the dumpling by pulling up the corners and pinching the pastry together until the seams are totally sealed. Repeat this process with the remaining squares.

Assemble the ingredients for the pecan streusel in a small bowl. Grease a baking sheet, or line it with parchment paper. Place the dumplings on the sheet and brush them with a bit more of the beaten egg. Top with the pecan streusel.

Bake for 15 minutes, then reduce heat to 350°F and bake for 25 minutes more or until lightly browned.

Make the icing by combining the confectioners' sugar, vanilla, and milk until you reach the proper consistency.

When the dumplings are done, let them cool to room temperature and drizzle them with icing before serving.

Nutrition:

Calories: 230

Fats 6.5g

Carbohydrates 44.6g

Fiber 2g

Protein 2.11g

Campfire S’mores

Preparation Time: 15 minutes

Cooking Time: 40 minutes

Servings: 9

Ingredients:

Graham Cracker Crust

2 cups graham cracker crumbs

¼ cup sugar

½ cup butter

½ teaspoon cinnamon

1 small package brownie mix (enough for an 8×8-inch pan), or use the brownie ingredients listed below.

Brownie Mix

½ cup flour

⅓ cup cocoa

¼ teaspoon baking powder

¼ teaspoon salt

½ cup butter

1 cup sugar

1 teaspoon vanilla

2 large eggs

S'mores Topping

9 large marshmallows

5 Hershey candy bars

4½ cups vanilla ice cream

½ cup chocolate sauce

Directions:

Preheat the oven to 350°F.

Mix the graham cracker crumbs, sugar, cinnamon and melted butter in a medium bowl. Stir until the crumbs and sugar have combined with the butter.

Line an 8×8-inch baking dish with parchment paper. Make sure to use enough so that you'll be able to lift the baked brownies out of the dish easily. Press the graham cracker mixture into the bottom of the lined pan.

Place pan in the oven to prebake the crust a bit while you are making the brownie mixture. First, sift (or mix) together the flour, cocoa, baking powder, and salt in a large bowl.

Melt the butter over medium heat in a large saucepan, then stir in the sugar and vanilla. Whisk in the eggs one at a time. Then whisk in the dry ingredients, followed by the nuts. Mix until smooth. Take the crust out of the oven, pour the mixture into it, and bake for 23–25 minutes. When brownies are done, remove from oven and let cool in the pan.

After the brownies have cooled completely, lift them out of the pan using the edges of the parchment paper. Be careful not to crack or break the brownies. Cut into individual slices.

When you are ready to serve, place a marshmallow on top of each brownie and broil in the oven until the marshmallow starts to brown. You can also microwave for a couple of seconds, but you won't get the browning that you would in the broiler.

Remove from the oven and top each brownie with half of a Hershey bar. Serve with ice cream and a drizzle of chocolate sauce.

Nutrition:

Calories: 280

Fats 6.8g

Carbohydrates 51g

Fiber 2g

Protein 2.5g

Copycat Levain Bakery Cookies

No need to wait in line for these copycat Levain Bakery Cookies

Preparation Time: 15 minutes

Servings: 15

Ingredients:

2 c. all-purpose flour

1 1/4 c. cake flour

2 tsp. baking powder

1/4 tsp. baking soda

1/4 tsp. kosher salt

1 c. (2 sticks) cold butter, cubed

2/3 c. packed brown sugar

2/3 c. granulated sugar

2 c. dark chocolate chips

1 c. very coarsely chopped walnuts, lightly toasted

2 large eggs, lightly beaten

Directions:

Line two large baking sheets with parchment paper. In a medium bowl, whisk together flours, baking powder, baking soda, and kosher salt.

In a large bowl using a hand mixer (or in the bowl of a stand mixer), cream cold butter on low speed until cubes lose half their shape, about 30 to 45 seconds. Add sugars and continue to cream briefly, 30 to 60 seconds more. Add chocolate and walnuts and beat until combined.

Gradually add flour mixture and beat to combine; mixture will be a bit crumbly. If any big pieces of butter remain, use hands to cut butter into smaller pieces. Add in eggs and beat until fully combined and smooth, forming a cohesive dough.

Portion large balls of dough, about 6 ounces or ¾ cup each. Place 4 balls of dough on each prepared tray and place in freezer. Let chill for 90 minutes.

When ready to bake, preheat oven to 375°. Place one empty baking sheet upside-down in oven and place one tray of frozen dough on top. Bake one sheet of cookies at a time, until edges and spots on top are golden, but insides are still slightly doughy, about 26 minutes.

Nutrition:

Calories: 790kcal

Fats: 40g

Carbohydrates: 98g

Protein: 13g

Olive Garden Peaches and Cream Cheesecake

Make the Olive Garden Peaches and Cream Cheesecake at home.

Preparation Time: 30 minutes

Cooking Time: 120 minutes

Servings: 16

Ingredients:

Sponge cake base

1 egg

1/3 cup sugar

1/4 teaspoon vanilla

1/4 cup all-purpose flour

1/4 teaspoon baking powder

1 pinch salt

2 tablespoons water

The Filling

32 ounces cream cheese softened

1 cup sugar

4 eggs

1 teaspoon all-purpose flour

1 teaspoon vanilla

1 cup sour cream

1/4 cup peach liqueur or peach Schnapps or reserved juice from canned peaches

2 cups canned peaches or firm peaches, sliced and drained well

Topping

1 pint whipping cream or equivalent

Directions:

The Base

Preheat oven to 375 degrees. Lightly grease base of 10″ springform pan. Beat whole egg in 1 and 1/2-quart bowl with mixer on high speed for 4 minutes to a thick yellow foam. Mix in sugar on low speed until smooth. Add flour, water, vanilla, baking powder, and salt. Mix on low speed until fully blended. Pour into springform pan; roll around until level. Bake 16 to 18 minutes on lowest oven rack. Cool to room temp.

The Filling

Preheat oven to 325 degrees. Mix cream cheese, sugar, eggs and flour with electric mixer on high until smooth. Add vanilla, sour cream and peach flavoring and mix on medium until smooth and thick. Fold in peach slices carefully; distribute evenly. Pour cheesecake filling onto cooled sponge cake base. Bake 70 minutes on lower oven rack. Turn off oven, open oven door to broil position and let cake remain 40 minutes. Cool to refrigerated temperature.

The Topping

Top with fresh whipped cream or equivalent and serve. Store up to 2 days in the fridge.

Nutrition:

Calories: 435kcal

Fats: 34g

Carbohydrates: 24g

Protein: 6g

Olive Garden's Favorite Recipes

Cobb Salad

This is among the most customary food in American culinary history. With its mixture of chicken, bacon, boiled eggs, blue cheese as properly as avocado, it is a severely enjoyable salad. Above with a Dijon mustard dressing, lemon juice, and Worcestershire sauce, it is so effortless to discover why the Cobb salad is an American favorite.

Preparation Time: 10 minutes

Cooking Time: 15 minutes

Servings: 4

Ingredients:

6 (14 oz.) rindless bacon rashers

1 large avocado, cut into one ½" pieces

½ lemon, juiced

2 Romaine lettuces, roughly chopped

3 ½ oz. blue cheese, crumbled

3 hard-boiled eggs, reduce into one ½" pieces

11 ½ oz. (2 cups) prepared chicken, reduce into ½" pieces

3 small Roma tomatoes, seeded, reduce into ½" portions

Chives, chopped, to serve

Lemon dressing

½ cup of olive oil

2 tablespoons white wine vinegar

½ lemon, juiced

2 garlic cloves, crushed

½ tsp white sugar

½ tsp Dijon mustard

1 tablespoon Worcestershire sauce

Directions:

Whisk the substances in a bowl until nicely mixed to make the dressing. Season with pepper and salt, then put aside;

Preheat grill to high. Place bacon rashers on an oven tray as nicely as a cook for four minutes every aspect or until golden and crisp;

Drain on the paper towel, then reduce into 0.40" portions Toss avocado in lemon juice;

Place lettuce leaves in a big bowl, prepare the avocado, blue cheese, eggs, bacon, tomatoes, and hen in rows in addition to the lettuce;

Drizzle with the lemon dressing as nicely as serve scattered with chives.

When you are ready to serve, place a marshmallow on top of each brownie and broil in the oven until the marshmallow starts to brown. You can also microwave for a couple of seconds, but you won't get the browning that you would in the broiler.

Remove from the oven and top each brownie with half of a Hershey bar. Serve with ice cream and a drizzle of chocolate sauce.

Nutrition:

Calories: 735

Fats 4.8g

Carbohydrates 70g

Fiber 5g

Protein 28g

Steakhouse Salad

Horseradish and steak sauce provide this hearty salad its steakhouse appeal. (Oh, as nicely as the strips of gentle beef sirloin steak, add to that.

Preparation Time: 10 minutes

Cooking Time: 30 minutes

Servings: 4

Ingredients:

½ (¾ lb.) red meat sirloin steak, ¾" thick

1 ⅓ tablespoon A1. original sauce

¼ cup of Kraft mayo with olive oil

¼ cup Kraft lite ranch dressing

1 ⅓ tablespoon Kraft horseradish

5 ⅓ cups loosely packed romaine lettuce, chopped

½ tomato, cut into wedges

½ small white onion, reduce into small wedges

⅓ cup Kraft two percent sharp cheddar cheese, shredded

Directions:

Heat grill to medium heat;

Grill steak three minutes Per side. Coat with half of the A.1. Sauce. Grill four to 5 minutes or until medium doneness (160° F), turning and once in a while coating with the relaxation of the A.1. Sauce;

The steak has to be now placed on a cutting board and carefully covered. Let it sit and stand for 5 minutes. Meanwhile, whisk mayo, dressing, and horseradish till combined;

Slice the steak across the grain into small slices. Carefully cowl platter with lettuce; top with tomatoes, meat, and onions. Drizzle with mayo mixture; sprinkle with cheese.

Nutrition:

Calories: 783

Fats 4.8g

Carbohydrates 60g

Fiber 5g

Protein 20g

Kookaburra Wings

Chicken wings are among the most famous snacks and appetizers, no longer just in the United States, but in almost every nook of the globe. Try this kookaburra wing recipe, and you will like it.

Preparation Time: 10 minutes

Cooking Time: 30 minutes

Servings: 4

Ingredients:

10 small poultry wings

48 oz. shortening

2 tablespoons of flour, all-purpose

1 tablespoon Kraft Macaroni and Cheese topping

1 ¼ teaspoons salt

1 teaspoon chili powder

¾ teaspoon black pepper, ground

½ teaspoon cayenne pepper

¼ teaspoon paprika

¼ teaspoon onion powder, granulated

¼ teaspoon garlic powder, granulated

⅛ teaspoon cumin powder

Dash ground clove

2 tablespoons Hot sauce

1 teaspoon water

Directions:

Preheat shortening (you might also use vegetable or canola oil) to 375° F;

Make the spiced breading for your wings using merging the wing masking components (flour thru clove) In a smooth medium bowl. Stir well;

Dip each wing, one at a period into the breading. Give anybody a light layer of things;

Arrange breaded wings on a plate and take a seat uncovered in the fridge for about 15 minutes;

When the shortening or oil is hot, lower the wings into it. Fry for 7 to 10 minutes or likely until the wings are brown;

While the wings are frying, combo the hot sauce as well as water in a bowl;

Drain the wings when they are finished for a 2d on a rack or paper towels;

Put the warm wings into a huge clear plastic container with a lid;

Put the sauce over the wings. Cover the pot and gently shake it to coat the wings with sauce;

Use tongs to get rid of the wings from the container;

Arrange on a plate with blue cheese sauce and celery sticks on the side.

Nutrition:

Calories: 375

Fats 8g

Carbohydrates 67.5g

Fiber 3g

Protein 7.5g

Spicy Volcano Shrimp

Delicious and light. Serve to sparkle with an inexperienced salad, rice, and clean melon or other fruits.

Preparation Time: 10 minutes

Cooking Time: 30 minutes

Servings: 4

Ingredients:

24 oz. raw jumbo shrimp

2 tablespoons sesame oil

½ cup soy sauce

2 teaspoons garlic, minced

1 cup orange marmalade

2 tablespoons chili powder

4 tablespoons inexperienced onions, chopped

2 teaspoons pink pepper flakes

2 teaspoons ginger, minced

2 tablespoons toasted sesame seeds

2 tablespoons roasted peanuts, chopped

Directions:

If shrimp are frozen thaw overnight in the fridge;

Set the final substances in a huge skillet, deliver to a boil as properly as simmer for 5 minutes approximately;

Toss in shrimp, simmer for 5 minutes, or until shrimp are opaque and pink;

Serve over hot rice of your choice;

Garnish with peanuts or sesame seeds.

Nutrition:

Calories: 291

Fats 17g

Carbohydrates 26.5g

Fiber 2g

Protein 7.5g

Slow-Roasted Prime Rib

An astonishing centerpiece for an excursion menu. This three-bone prime rib roast gets heaped with a big pile of smashed garlic, butter, and clean herbs, then gradual cooked it in a decreased oven for no less than 2 hours, until the meat gets meltingly tender, as nicely as the herbs as nicely as garlic infuse it thru and through.

Preparation Time: 20 minutes

Cooking Time: 1 hour 30 minutes

Servings: 4

Ingredients:

3 (2 lbs.) bone pork rib roast

3 tablespoons fleur de sel

1 ½ tablespoon cracked black pepper

1 tablespoon of olive oil, extra-virgin

8 sprigs rosemary

8 sprigs thyme

10 garlic cloves, smashed

3 tablespoons of butter, unsalted, cut into ½" cubes

Directions:

Remove the red meat out of the fridge two hours earlier than cooking so that it can come to room temperature.

Season the meat after 30 minutes, on all facets with the fleur de sel and cracked black pepper;

Place and function a rack in the center of the oven and warmness oven to 325° F;

Turn on the exhaust fan. Heat a 12" skillet overheat that is excessive for 1 minute;

Swirl the olive oil in and, when the oil throws off smoke, set the red meat in the pan, and burn it on all of the exterior facets until properly browned 6 to 8 minutes total. Try using a set of tongs to flip the beef; be cautious of splattering oil;

With two units of tongs, switch the meat, bone facet down, to a roasting rack set in a small roasting pan;

Arrange butter, garlic, thyme, and the rosemary evenly;

Roast the beef, while basting every 30 minutes with a baster until a thermometer inserted into the middle reads 120° F to 125° F for rare, about two hours. Cook to 130°/135° F for medium-rare (about 2:15 hours), 140° F to 145° F for reasonable (approximately 2:30 hours). Let the beef rest at least fifteen minutes earlier than carving.

Nutrition:

Calories: 407

Fats 8g

Carbohydrates 34.6g

Fiber 3g

Protein 21g

Sauteed' Shrooms

These mushrooms are honestly the quintessential topping for those sorts of steak. Also awesome on baked potatoes. They're that great.

Preparation Time: 10 minutes

Cooking Time: 10 minutes

Servings: 4

Ingredients:

3 tablespoons olive oil

3 tablespoons butter, softened

1 lb. button mushrooms, sliced

1 clove garlic, sliced thinly

1 tablespoon white wine

1 tablespoon teriyaki sauce

¼ teaspoon garlic powder

Black pepper to taste

Directions:

Heat coconut oil as well as butter in a large smooth saucepan over medium heat;

Cook and stir black pepper, garlic powder, teriyaki sauce, cooking wine, garlic, and mushrooms in the warm oil as properly as butter until mushrooms are gently browned, about 5 minutes;

Reduce the warmness and simmer until mushrooms are smooth and gentle, five to eight extra minutes.

Nutrition:

Calories: 42

Fats 0.11g

Carbohydrates 4g

Fiber 3g

Protein 3.7g

Steamed Lobster Tail

This simple recipe for steamed lobster tails will be the best way to ensure the best lobster.

Preparation Time: 2 minutes

Cooking Time: 10 minutes

Servings: 4

Ingredients:

1 tablespoon sea salt

4 (6 oz.) lobster tails

½ cup butter, melted

Directions:

Pour approximately 1" of water in the backside section of a large pot and then deliver to a boil;

Add the salt and put a steamer insert inside the pan, so it's simply above the water level;

Arrange and set the lobster tails on the rack and cautiously cover the container;

Steam and carefully cover for eight minutes. And do no longer peek;

Serve to sparkle with butter, melted.

Nutrition:

Calories: 106

Fats 0.9g

Carbohydrates 2g

Fiber 4g

Protein 20g

Smoked Mozzarella Fondue

Try this easy Olive Garden copy cat fondue.

Preparation Time: 5 minutes

Cooking Time: 30 minutes

Servings: 6-8

Ingredients:

8 oz. cream cheese, softened to room temperature

1 c. smoked mozzarella

1 c. provolone

1/2 c. freshly grated Parmesan

1/3 c. sour cream

1/2 tsp. dried thyme

1/2 tsp. Italian seasoning

1/4 tsp. red pepper flakes

kosher salt

Freshly ground black pepper

1 small tomato, chopped

1 tbsp. parsley, finely chopped

Directions:

Preheat oven to 350° F.

In a large bowl, combine cream cheese, cheeses, sour cream, thyme, Italian seasoning and red pepper flakes. Stir together until smooth and fully combined. Season with salt and pepper.

Transfer cheese mixture into a small skillet. Bake until cheese is bubbling, around 20-25 minutes. Broil if desired.

Garnish with tomato and parsley and serve with baguette.

Nutrition:

Calories: 406

Fats 49g

Carbohydrates 2g

Fiber 4g

Protein 20g

Breadsticks

The Most Famous And Simple Olive Garden Recipe: Breadstick

Preparation Time: 25 minutes

Cooking Time: 12 minutes

Servings: 4

Ingredients

2 tablespoons white sugar

¼ (0.25 oz.) package active dry yeast

¼ cup of warm water

1 cup all-purpose flour

⅓ tablespoon vegetable oil

¼ egg

1 pinch salt

2 tablespoons butter, melted

1 pinch garlic salt

2 tablespoons Parmesan cheese, shredded

Directions:

Take a small bowl and add 1 ½ teaspoons sugar, ¼ cup warm water, and yeast;

Mix these ingredients well then leave them for 5 minutes;

Meanwhile, mix flour with remaining sugar, salt, egg, and oil;

Mix well and stir in yeast mixture;

Knead this dough for 8 minutes then transfer to a bowl greased with cooking oil;

Cover the dough with a damp cloth and place it in a warm place;

After 40 minutes, knead the dough again;

Divide the dough into 4 to 6-inches ropes and place them in a greased baking sheet;

Keep each rope 2 inches apart and cover them with plastic wrap.

Leave them for 25 minutes at room temperature;

Meanwhile, set the oven temperature at 400 degrees F;

Remove the plastic wrap off the baking sheet and bake the dough for 12 minutes until golden brown;

Meanwhile, mix butter with garlic in a bowl then brush over the breadsticks liberally;

Drizzle parmesan cheese on top of each bread;

Serve fresh;

To keep the breadsticks fresh, keep them in a sealed jar or wrapped in plastic.

Nutrition:

Calories: 230

Fats 10g

Carbohydrates 9.3g

Fiber 1g

Protein 7.3g

Sodium 120g

McDonald's Favorite Recipes

McDonald's Hamburger

Recreate the McDonald's Hamburger at home in no time at all.

Preparation Time: 2 minutes

Cooking Time: 10 minutes

Servings: 8

Ingredients:

Burger Seasoning

1 tablespoon salt

2 teaspoon ground black pepper

1/4 teaspoon Accent seasoning (optional)

Hamburger Ingredients

1 pound ground chuck

8 hamburger buns

2 tablespoons dehydrated onions

16 dill pickle slices

4 tablespoons ketchup

3 tablespoons mustard

Directions:

Burger seasoning

Combine salt, pepper, and accent in a small bowl. Use this to season the meat. You will not use all of this. You can store the remaining and use another time.

Dehydrated Onions

Place the dehydrated onions into a small bowl and add 2 tablespoons of warm water. These will hydrate and be ready by the time you finish cooking the burgers.

Hamburger Instructions

For this recipe I like to use a griddle, it is important for the juices to float away from the burger while cooking. If you do not have one, you can use a very large skillet. Preheat the griddle to 375 degrees.

Form 8 small round patties with the ground chuck. Place the patties on the hot grill. Use a spatula and press the patty into the grill for 4 to 5 seconds to sear in the juices.

You know you have pressed the patty into the grill hard enough when you have to scrape it from the griddle. Season the patties liberally.

Cook the patties on both sides. When you flip the burger, season the other side well. When the burgers are done place the buns on the hot griddle and toast the buns until they begin to brown.

To assemble the burgers you will want to place 5 small squirts of mustard on the bottom bun. Follow the mustard with 5 larger squirts of ketchup. Add some onions, and a dill pickle slice or two. Place the hamburger patty on top of the pickle. Place the top bun on top of meat patty.

Cheeseburger

If you would like to make a McDonald's cheeseburger, simply add a slice of American cheese to the burger patty once you have flipped it over. Cook for another minute or so, and remove from the grill. Dress the burger with ketchup, mustard, pickle slices and onion.

Nutrition:

Calories: 280

Fats: 13g

Carbohydrates: 25g

Protein: 14g

Fiber: 1g

Sodium: 1380mg

Copycat Big Mac

As you know, Big Mac's have three layers of buns. It's so easy to make your own version.

Preparation Time: 2 minutes

Cooking Time: 10 minutes

Servings: 5

Ingredients:

1 1/2 pounds ground chuck

1/2 teaspoon salt

1/4 teaspoon black pepper

1 tablespoon of butter

¼ cup special sauce

5 slices of American cheese

1 tablespoon minced onion

15 dill pickle slices

Directions:

In a bowl combine ground chuck and salt and pepper. Shape meat into 10 meat patties. Shape patties somewhat thin. Set a griddle to 350 degrees. Place meat on the griddle and cook for 3 to 4 minutes. Season with a sprinkle of salt and pepper. Flip burgers and cook for an additional 3 to 4 minutes on each side, or until juices from the meat run clear.

Spread softened butter on cut sides of bun and place on griddle until the bread begins to brown. Flip the middle bun and allow to toast on both sides.

Build the burger by starting at the bottom. The bottom bun, Big Mac sauce, onions, lettuce, cheese, hamburger patty, and the middle bun. Spread the Big Mac sauce, onion, lettuce, hamburger patty, two or three pickle slices, and finally the top bun.

Nutrition:

Calories: 445

Fats: 36g

Carbohydrates: 1g

Protein: 27g

Copycat Egg McMuffin

Learn how to make a McDonalds Egg McMuffin at home with this easy copycat recipe. Find out the secret to making perfect egg rings for a breakfast sandwich.

Preparation Time: 2 minutes

Cooking Time: 10 minutes

Servings: 4

Ingredients:

4 tablespoons softened butter butter has divided uses

4 English Muffins

4 slices Canadian Bacon

4 eggs

1/2 cup water

4 slices American cheese

Directions:

Split open English Muffins and place them into a toaster, toast the English Muffins.

In a non-stick skillet over medium heat, cook Candian bacon on both sides for about 1 to 2 minutes in two teaspoons of butter. The bacon should begin to just brown.

While the Canadian bacon is cooking, remove the English muffins from the toaster and spread softened butter on both halves.

Place the 1 slice of Canadian bacon on each English Muffin bottom.

Add about 1 tablespoon of butter to the same skillet where you cooked the bacon.

Place the quart-sized canning lids screw size up (or you can use an egg ring) into the skillet.

Spray the canning lid with non-stick spray. Crack an egg into each of the rings.

Break the yolk with a folk. Pour about 1/2 cup of water into the skillet, and place a lid on top. Cook until the eggs are set, it should take about two minutes.

Gently remove the eggs from the rings, and place one egg on each piece of Canadian bacon.

Top each egg with one slice of American cheese, top cheese with the top of the English muffin.

Wrap each egg McMuffin with foil or parchment paper. Wait about 30 seonds before serving.

Nutrition:

Calories: 420

Fats: 25g

Carbohydrates: 28g

Protein: 20g

Fiber: 2g

McDonald's Cheddar Melt

The beloved sandwich of the 90s is alive and well, thanks to this copycat recipe.

Preparation Time: 15 minutes

Cooking Time: 10 minutes

Servings: 2

Ingredients:

3 tbsp. butter

3 tbsp. all-purpose flour

1 1/2 c. milk

1 c. shredded Cheddar

kosher salt

Freshly ground black pepper

2 burger patties

1/2 small onion, finely chopped

2 tbsp. teriyaki sauce

2 rye buns

Directions:

In a saucepan over medium heat, melt butter. Add flour and whisk until totally combined. Cook until golden, 1 minute, then pour in milk and whisk until completely combined. Let thicken 3 minutes. Add cheddar and whisk until combined and creamy. Season with salt and pepper. Keep sauce on low heat while you prep the rest of the burger.

In a large skillet over medium-high heat, heat oil. Add burger patties and season with salt and pepper. Cook 4 minutes per side for medium rare. Set aside.

Add onions to burger fat in skillet and sauté until tender, 6 minutes, then add teriyaki sauce and stir until combined.

Assemble burger: On a rye bun bottom, place burger patty and top with cheese sauce and teriyaki onions.

Nutrition:

Calories: 420

Fats: 25g

Carbohydrates: 28g

Protein: 20g

Fiber: 2g

McDonald's Oreo McFlurry

Enjoy a McDonald's Oreo McFlurry even more at home!

Preparation Time: 5 minutes

Servings: 1

Ingredients:

2 cups vanilla ice cream

2 tablespoons whole milk

4 Oreo cookies

Directions:

Place ice cream and milk into a blender, and puree ice cream and milk together.

Crumble Oreo cookies into the blender, then pulse the blender a few times to mix in the cookies.

Pour into a glass and enjoy!

Nutrition:

Calories: 790kcal

Fats: 40g

Carbohydrates: 98g

Protein: 13g

Fiber: 3g

McDonald's McCafe Caramel Cappuccino

You don't need to wait in the drive-thru to enjoy this McCafe Specialty

Preparation Time: 5 minutes

Servings: 1

Ingredients:

6 ounces coffee strong, or two shots of espresso

1/2 cup milk (the lower the fat content the better, it will froth more)

2 tablespoons caramel ice cream topping, divided use

2 tablespoons whipped cream garnish

Directions:

In a large warm coffee mug, pour in the coffee. Add 1 tablespoon of caramel syrup Add in the warmed milk stir. Top with whipped cream if desired, and then drizzle over the remaining caramel syrup.

Nutrition:

Calories: 212kcal

Fats: 4g

Carbohydrates: 29g

Protein: 5g

Conversion Tables

Since this book aims to make Italian cuisine known and spread all over the world, we believe it useful to indicate in this initial section some primary guidelines to adequately convert the units of measurement presented in the various recipes with those possibly used in other countries.

The unit of measure conversion table is essential in the kitchen when you want to prepare a recipe measured according to a standard different from what you are used to

The recipes are all expressed according to the decimal metric system, but some readers may need to transform them into local measurement systems.

Indeed, some mathematics may be needed initially, but even more, a little logic is necessary because a cup of liquids will weigh differently from a cup of solids, and the same happens with ounces that can measure solid and liquid ingredients.

COOKING CONVERSION CHART

Measurement

CUP	ONCES	MILLILITERS	TABLESPOONS
8 cup	64 oz	1895 ml	128
6 cup	48 oz	1420 ml	96
5 cup	40 oz	1180 ml	80
4 cup	32 oz	960 ml	64
2 cup	16 oz	480 ml	32
1 cup	8 oz	240 ml	16
3/4 cup	6 oz	177 ml	12
2/3 cup	5 oz	158 ml	11
1/2 cup	4 oz	118 ml	8
3/8 cup	3 oz	90 ml	6
1/3 cup	2.5 oz	79 ml	5.5
1/4 cup	2 oz	59 ml	4
1/8 cup	1 oz	30 ml	3
1/16 cup	1/2 oz	15 ml	1

Temperature

FAHRENHEIT	CELSIUS
100 °F	37 °C
150 °F	65 °C
200 °F	93 °C
250 °F	121 °C
300 °F	150 °C
325 °F	160 °C
350 °F	180 °C
375 °F	190 °C
400 °F	200 °C
425 °F	220 °C
450 °F	230 °C
500 °F	260 °C
525 °F	274 °C
550 °F	288 °C

Weight

IMPERIAL	METRIC
1/2 oz	15 g
1 oz	29 g
2 oz	57 g
3 oz	85 g
4 oz	113 g
5 oz	141 g
6 oz	170 g
8 oz	227 g
10 oz	283 g
12 oz	340 g
13 oz	369 g
14 oz	397 g
15 oz	425 g
1 lb	453 g

Conclusion

When you are on a budget and sometimes feel too lazy to put on shoes, dining out every day is not possible, so we found the best way to get you the restaurant! We have the lowdown on the best copycat recipes. If you feel inspired for more home-cooked meals, attempt any of the recipes given in this book to filled your cravings. Copycat recipes are everywhere for popular restaurant meals. To be sure, their authenticity is well known – industries recipes are always under strict supervision and key – but the taste buds know what it's like going on, and specific recipes come close to the originals. There are plenty of copycat recipes, and, luckily, they're not complicated. In reality, they can make with all items that you either already had or possibly purchased last week. This book has many dishes to try and enjoy these easy and tasty dishes at home whenever you want.

This book has excellent dishes for every event of the day, as well as your craving. You can try the best copycat classic entrees dishes like Margherita Chicken, Fiesta Lime Chicken, Panda Express's copycat beef and broccoli, and many more delicious recipes for your start of the day. There have been vegetarian and non-vegetarian recipes given in this book as far as lunch and dinner are concerned. You can try as per your choices and taste in the middle and end of the day. Whether it's Olive Garden's Pasta e Fagioli, DIY California Quinoa Salad from Whole Foods, and PF Chang's Hot and Sour Soup, you have it all here if your preference is have some veggies. And suppose you like to enjoy some meaty recipes. In that case, you can try the copycat Swordfish with lemon and tarragon, steamed lobster tails, Slow-Roasted Prime Rib, Chili's baby back ribs, and many more perfect recipes for your non-vegetarian lunch and dinner.

The meal is incomplete without soups in your menu. So, if you have been craving to have your favorite restaurant soup, you have many copycat recipes. Try Olive Garden's Creamy Zuppa Toscana, Panera's Broccoli cheddar soup, Outback's Baked Potato Soup, pasta e Fagioli from the olive garden, and other soups to complete your meal. It's always best to have some healthy and light salads in your diet to balance your nutritional requirements to stay healthy. So why not try the salad recipes given in this book. Olive Garden's Salad and Creamy Dressing, Cobb salad, Steakhouse salad, Garlic-shrimp Caesar salad, and many more copycat salad recipes would make your day.

In the end, it's time to satisfy our cravings with some desserts. Try Cherry Chocolate Cobbler, Double Fudge Coca Cola Cake, Chocolate Pecan Pie, Pumpkin Custard with Gingersnaps, and many more dessert recipes to discover in this book. And what better option than to try some of your favorite restaurants' recipes all by yourself. Try kookaburra wing, Spicy Volcano Shrimp, Sauteed' Shrooms, and many other recipes. It's the right moment to put your own on your chef hat and have ideal cooking and eating time with your family and friends.

CPSIA information can be obtained
at www.ICGtesting.com
Printed in the USA
LVHW052329020321
680389LV00028B/1350

9 781802 085143